Land Navigation
Hand~~book~~

The Sierra Club Outdoor Activities Guides

BACKCOUNTRY SKIING: *The Sierra Club Guide to Skiing off the Beaten Track*, by Lito Tejada-Flores

BIKE TOURING: *The Sierra Club Guide to Outings on Wheels*, by Raymond Bridge

CAVING: *The Sierra Club Guide to Spelunking*, by Lane Larson and Peggy Larson

THE COMPLETE BICYCLE COMMUTER: *The Sierra Club Guide to Wheeling to Work*, by Hal Zina Bennett

EXPLORING UNDERWATER: *The Sierra Club Guide to Scuba and Snorkeling*, by John L. Culliney and Edward S. Crockett

LAND NAVIGATION HANDBOOK: *The Sierra Club Guide to Map and Compass*, revised and updated, by W. S. Kals

SIMPLE FOODS FOR THE PACK: *The Sierra Club Guide to Delicious Natural Foods for the Trail*, completely revised and updated, by Claudia Axcell, Diana Cooke and Vikki Kinmont

STARTING SMALL IN THE WILDERNESS: *The Sierra Club Guide for Families*, by Marlyn Doan

WALKING SOFTLY IN THE WILDERNESS: *The Sierra Club Guide to Backpacking*, revised and updated, by John Hart

WEATHERING THE WILDERNESS: *The Sierra Club Guide to Practical Meteorology*, by William E. Reifsnyder

WILDWATER: *The Sierra Club Guide to Kayaking and Whitewater Boating*, by Lito Tejada-Flores

Land Navigation Handbook

*The Sierra Club Guide
to Map
and Compass*

W. S. Kals

Sierra Club Books · San Francisco

The Sierra Club, founded in 1892 by John Muir, has devoted itself to the study and protection of the Earth's scenic and ecological resources—mountains, wetlands, woodlands, wild shores and rivers, deserts and plains. The publishing program of the Sierra Club offers books to the public as a nonprofit educational service in the hope that they may enlarge the public's understanding of the Club's basic concerns. The point of view expressed in each book, however, does not necessarily represent that of the Club. The Sierra Club has some sixty chapters coast to coast, in Canada, Hawaii, and Alaska. For information about how you may participate in its programs to preserve wilderness and the quality of life, please address inquiries to Sierra Club, 85 Second Street, San Francisco, CA 94105.

http://www.sierraclub.org/books

Library of Congress Cataloging in Publication Data
Kals, W. S.
Land navigation handbook
Includes index.
1. Orientation. 2. Maps. 3. Navigation. I. Title.
GV200.4.K34 1983 796.5 82-16917
ISBN 0-87156-331-2

Cover design by Pushpin Studios

Book design by Drake Jordan

Printed in the United States of America on acid-free paper containing a minimum of 50% recovered waste paper, of which at least 10% of the fiber content is post-consumer waste

20 19 18 17 16 15 14

Contents

1.
Land
Navigation

I fully expect some purist to accuse me of polluting the language by talking about "land navigation." The word *navigation* means guiding a ship through water. Now take away the water. Then take away the ship. Next add a pair of feet and you have roughly defined my subject.

The feet may be hiking, skiing, snowshoeing, or be cramped under you in a canoe.

The guidance I'll discuss for these and other outdoor activities is close to what marine navigation is about. Both kinds of navigation answer these questions: Can I get there from here? By which route? How long will it take? Where are we now? Where else could we go from here? What mountain (or whatever) is that over there?

Some of us learned navigation the way a foal learns horse business, by trotting alongside mother. At times you may have learned the kangaroo way, by being carried along. Later you may have navigated by watching the heels of the person in front of you.

Many hikers never get past that simple technique. All it needs, as author Harvey Manning points out, is skill in boot identification, so you won't follow a stranger up the wrong mountain at a trail junction.

But what'll you do when the boots disappear around the corner? Or when they themselves are lost?

Don't worry, there's hope for you. Lift up thine eyes. You'll probably notice that the boots ahead have been walking on a trail.

One authority estimates that 90 percent of all foot travel is on trails. My highly unscientific survey makes me think that figure is considerably higher in both the eastern and western United States.

And if you looked in summer, when most traveling is done, you'd notice that most trails are rather well marked. The footway itself is clearly blazed by the hundreds of Vibram soles that have passed before you. Out West, horseshoes add to the markings.

Some trails have been marked by blazes. These axe marks don't help the trees; after a few years of scarring and weathering, they don't help the wayfarer much either. Bright paint marks, renewed when necessary, are better.

The ones used in the Alps are especially good. They are framed in white, so you see a white-green-white band that's a lot more visible than just a green or even a blue or red one. A notice board at the railroad station tells you what color is used on the trail you want.

Very useful. But not as ingenious as the Appalachian Trail system, which uses a double marker to tell you to wake up wherever the trail forks or radically changes direction.

One difficulty in walking by markings and footway only is that you never know how long it'll take you. If you are lucky enough to find a sign at the trailhead giving the time to your destination, I suggest you double the time until you establish a more accurate factor. If the sign gives the distance rather than the time, count on making no more than a mile to a mile-and-a-half (one and a half to two and a half kilometers) per hour. If you carry cameras, children, or both, you won't even make that.

But you'll get there eventually—in good summer weather.

Fog may not let you see the next marker. Snow wipes out all signs of a footway quickly, surprisingly quickly. Wind-driven snow obliterates blazes, paint, and other markers. If you try to retrace your steps—as you should—you'll find that the landscape looks completely unfamiliar. That's unless you turned around often on the way in and memorized what the world looks like when you walk the other way.

You should do that even if you have no intention whatever of returning by the same trail. Weather, a washed away footbridge or some minor mishap may force you to execute that popular and highly recommended course change: a 180° turn.

Following marked trails is not advanced navigation, but it beats heel watching.

It won't be long before you'll want a map; a map that lets you figure out your own routes and how long they should take at your pace. Often by itself, a map without a compass also tells you where you are.

That sounds as if a map could solve most problems of navigation. Within some limits, it does.

You could walk the Appalachian Trail from Springer Mountain, Georgia, to Mount Katahdin, Maine without a map. But how would you find the post office where your next supply of freeze-dried food and mail is waiting? How would you even know where to have things sent without a map?

Maps alone will also get you halfway across Europe, from Spain by way of France, Switzerland, and Austria to Hungary. Again, you could probably find the trail without them. But there it is not just a matter of freeze-dried food; the maps tell you where the huts are and whether they serve meals (typically a choice of three main courses, with beer or wine if you like) or only offer a stove for you to cook on.

The next chapter may tell you more about maps than you want to know. But this book is not only for people just advancing from following boots. It should also serve as refresher for people who have become a bit rusty in land navigation. And I hope even experts will find things in this book they did not know. (People with experience in small craft navigation will find new applications for things they already know.)

I'll show you how to decode most map symbols, and how to read distance, height, and direction from a map. I'll help you answer such questions as: How steep is the trail? How long will it take me uphill, and downhill?

Once you are familiar with hiking maps the whole world becomes your playground. You'll be able to sight-read maps in Canada, the Andes, the Himalayas, or the Austrian Alps. The differences in details are small and are usually stated on the maps themselves.

The Austrian map, for example, will show the symbols used to distinguish between a cable car, a chair lift, a ski tow, and a freight lift that may or may not carry your pack to the hut. The fact that it uses meters and kilometers rather than feet and miles will hardly bother you.

By the time you have reached the subject of reading directions from the map—if not earlier—you'll want a compass.

There are odd situations when a compass by itself lets you navigate. But in general, land navigation, like basic marine navigation, is mainly map and compass work. And map and compass are the only tools you'll need. You'll often find a dime store ruler useful, and sometimes a pencil stub.

Binoculars, although not counted as navigational tools by most writers, are as helpful in spotting and identifying the next marker as they are in marine navigation.

If you have ever had anything to do with magnetic compasses, you may recall hazily that hardly anywhere does the needle point where you'd expect it to. I strongly suggest you spend a few extra dollars and get a compass that, once set, lets you forget about the problem until you move to an other area. But for readers who'd rather blow their bucks on freeze-dried shrimp cocktails, I have provided several methods for dealing with that compass problem. Among them you should be able to find one that repels you less than the others.

A compass, once that foible is taken care of, helps you solve navigational problems such as: If I'm here— say on the peak of a mountain—what mountain is that over there? Or often more usefully: Over there is Mount Onthemap; where on the Appalachian Trail am I?

You'll read about *position lines,* a concept that ties these and other navigational problems together. Advanced marine navigators may call them lines of position—Lops for short.

With an altimeter to measure your elevation, you'll learn to fix your position on the map even when you can't see past the tips of your skis.

No book on land navigation is complete without instructions for finding directions from the sky. I won't disappoint you. You'll also read about methods that work where you lose sight of the polestar in the tropics, and in the Southern Hemisphere.

In the last chapter I have collected some useful terms, concepts, and tricks. Many of them come from orienteering, a competitive sport that combines running with map and compass work.

Orienteering, started at the end of the last century by military messengers in Scandinavia, has become popular in the United States, Canada, Great Britain, and some twenty other countries.

Orienteering competitions are usually staged in hilly woods, but the tips given in the last chapter are useful outside competitions, and in any terrain.

I've kept the most important technique for last.

I'm indebted for it to my younger daughter. When she was about ten, she was about to make her first solo trip across the continent, with change of airline in Seattle and New York. I went over all the things that could go wrong for her. Then I had one more worry.

"What'll you do if something comes up that we haven't discussed?"

Her answer has helped me in several sticky situations: "I'll stop to think what an intelligent person would do in my place."

2.
Maps and
Map Symbols

Everybody knows what a map is, but I have yet to see a satisfactory definition. One dictionary calls it a "representation of the earth's surface." That's not wide enough; what about a map of the moon or of Mars? The definition is also too wide. "A representation of the surface of the earth or a celestial body" makes it more awkward, but hardly any better.

Another dictionary refers to a representation of "whole or part of an area." To me part of an area is an area. But how large an area? A representation of where the radishes and broccoli are planted in your yard is hardly a map.

And what does the dictionary mean by the word *representation?* Perhaps the word *flat* should be in the definition to distinguish maps from globes and from models you may see in the visitors' center of a National Park that show the area with mountains and valleys in three dimensions. But this criterion also runs into trouble. You may have seen miniature relief maps on which the mountains are raised just a little above the plain. Their makers call them maps.

Most of us are agreed that the earth is almost a sphere. How to show that three-dimensional surface, quite apart from the wrinkles formed by mountains and valleys, on a flat sheet of paper is the job of the mapmaker. The problem has been solved so well that you can forget all about it when using the maps discussed in this book.

The viewpoint of the representation should also be mentioned in the definition. You have probably seen paintings of mountains with chair lifts and hiking trails or ski runs shown in perspective. The artist seems to have stood on a mountain—real or imagined—looking North or South or whatever. Maps always show the land seen from directly above.

Of course, they also show it greatly reduced in size. A map the size of Rocky Mountain National Park— about 21 by 26 miles (34 by 42 kilometers)—would be awkward to handle. A sheet roughly 28 by 38 inches (71 by 97 centimeters) is handier.

To be really useful, directions on maps should be related to directions in nature. Trails that cross at right angles should be shown crossing at the same angles on the map. And it should be possible to read geographic directions from a map. By custom geographic North on maps is at the top. A point that in nature is directly North of another one will be directly above it on the map.

Also, distances on maps should be related to distances in nature. Points two miles apart should be shown twice as far apart on the map as points only one mile apart.

Until a few years ago I could have used the word *drawing* (or perhaps *precision drawing*) to replace the mushy word *representation*. But now the United States Geological Survey publishes some maps that are not drawn. These *orthophoto* maps are photographic maps. (The *ortho-* part of the word refers to straightening the original aerial photos to minimize distortion.)

While all original maps now start from aerial photographs, most are not photographs themselves but drawings based on photographs with graphic symbols—say a tent for a campsite—added. The overlapping aerial photographs of mapmakers are supplemented by ground surveys that locate control points within the area to be mapped and measure the precise elevation of many points. Some points may serve as both horizontal and vertical controls.

Here's how maps are made from aerial photographs. The photograph is projected onto a sheet of paper on which the control points have been accurately plotted. The size of the projected image is then adjusted, and the drawing shifted until two photographed control points fall exactly on the marks on the paper, just as a photographer adjusts his enlarger for size and moves the paper holder to get the image where he wants it.

Only rarely will the other control points project right onto their marks on the drawing. Why? Everyone who has ever taken a photograph of a tall building can answer that: tilting the camera to get the top of the building into the picture makes the building in the photograph narrower at the top than at the bottom. Perhaps the plane's nose was up, tilting the camera and making the distance between marks ahead less than it should have been.

Unlike simple photographic enlargers, the projectors used in mapmaking let you tilt the negative (and the table) to correct for that. On the first try the marks will probably be closer to the drawn ones, but not quite in place yet. Perhaps one wing of the plane was some-what higher than the other at the time of the exposure. If the plane was flying North, a tilt in the East-West direction of negative and table will correct that.

Buildings, roads, railroads, and other man-made features, all of which will be printed in black, are then traced. This is also the time to add place names and legends. For example, a radio tower is marked, like other landmarks, as a dot in the center of a small circle. It's certainly a fine landmark, but of little use without the legend that tells you it is not a chimney, a water tower, a flagpole, or a windmill.

Place names may be on file on older maps, but much information has to be gathered by field investigation. For example, is the roof in the photograph attached to

a building where people live, in which case it'll be a
solid black on the map, or to a business, which would
be shown by black shading?

Next come creeks, banks of rivers, and other water-
ways, as well as lakes and ponds. All these features go
on a printing plate that will be inked blue.

On the plate to be inked red are drawn the highways, survey lines, and edges of fields.

On the plate to be inked green are drawn the areas
covered with trees.

Information is added in the margins of the map,
such as the identification of the area, and everything is
checked. Then the map is printed in each of the colors,
in exact register with the first one printed, on the same
sheet. Trimming the margins finishes the map.

For many of my readers—hikers, backpackers, fishermen, hunters, skiers—and for people planning highways, pipelines, and so on, such a map is not good
enough. What they need is a *topographic* map.

It does not help a bit to know that this word comes
from the Greek words *topos,* "a place," and *graphein,* "to
write or draw." All maps describe or draw places. Topographic maps clearly show the topography, the ups
and downs of the landscape, as opposed to *planimetric*
maps, which show the land as though it were all at
one level.

The map whose development from aerial photographs you just read about is a planimetric map. So are
political maps in an atlas, which might show the
United States in green, Canada in pink, Mexico in purple, and so on.

Other maps in the same atlas—physical maps—use
colors to show elevations above sea level. Everything
between sea level and 500 feet may be bluish green;
above that but below 1000 feet, a lighter shade of the
same tint; 1000 to 2000 feet, beige; 2000 to 5000 feet, a
lighter beige; 5000 to 10,000 feet, yellow; and everything above that, white.

To make a planimetric map into a topographic map
requires one more color—brown, for example—to be
printed in perfect register with the other colors.

The process that translates aerial photographs into squiggles for the brown printing plate is based on your great grandmother's gadget the stereopticon. Looking through that device at photographs taken with two cameras (or one camera with two lenses side by side), Victorians could see Albert Hall, the Taj Mahal, the Matterhorn, or the fat lady from the circus in three dimensions.

A more recent popular application of stereoscopic vision was 3-D movies. Two cameras were used to shoot the picture; the film taken with one was projected in red, the other in blue. The patrons were given spectacles with a red filter for one eye and a blue one for the other. Wearing these specs you could thrill to a stomach-knotting rollercoaster ride or watch a pair of lions eat their way through a sleeping car full of people, all seemingly in three dimensions.

In the production of topographic maps, two aerial photographs taken miles apart are projected through red and blue filters. The operator of the sophisticated stereo-plotter looks through red and blue glasses.

He first adjusts both images for tilt of the plane fore and aft and wing to wing at the time the pictures were taken. Then he looks for one of the vertical control points. He raises or lowers the table onto which the images are projected until the two images of the control point fuse into one.

By the laws of optics, all points at the same elevation, and only these points, will now also fuse. The operator then traces a line connecting all these points. That line becomes the contour line at the elevation of the vertical control point. He then raises the table a predetermined distance and traces the next contour.

You'll read about these contours in more detail in Chapter 4, "Height from the Map." For now you may just want to look at the fold-out map just inside the back cover of this book and glance at the wiggly brown lines. That should give you a better feel for what makes a topographic map than any dictionary definition.

Topographic maps are very accurate. Here are the standards of accuracy for U.S. topo maps on the scale of the fold-out map in the back of this book, the very popular 7½' series in which one inch on the map corresponds to 2000 feet in the field.

Horizontally. No more than 10 percent of well-defined map points may be more than 40 feet from their true position. On the maps, this means 1/50 inch (about ½ millimeter).

Vertically. No more than 10 percent of the elevations derived from contour lines may be more than one-half contour interval off. The contour interval—the difference from one printed contour to the next—on the fold-out map, as on many of these maps in mountainous regions, is 40 feet; 90 percent of all points checked on these maps must be within 20 feet (6 meters) of their true height above sea level. In flat country, where the contour interval typically is 10 feet, they'd have to be within 5 feet (1½ meters).

That's certainly accurate enough for hiking, skiing, hunting, fishing. And it's good enough to plan a road, a real estate development, a ski lift, or a pipeline.

Do topographic maps like the sample in this book tell the whole truth? No, and you would not want them to. You wouldn't want them cluttered with every chicken coop, woodshed, and outhouse. They show that an area is not wooded, but is it bare rock or meadow? The map does not say.

And all maps show things that you won't see in the landscape. Have you ever seen a meridian of longitude, or a parallel of latitude? Or the lines that enclose a section of land, or form borders of counties or national forests?

Also, time makes liars out of maps. By the time they are printed they are already partially out of date. An area is not wooded anymore, a road has been straightened, a railroad track has been torn up and sold for scrap. New houses have been built, a new dam has created a lake, a mangrove swamp has been filled and seeded with townhouses. The quickest and easiest way to show these changes is to overprint existing maps. The corrections, printed in purple, are based on interpretation of the latest aerial photographs without field investigation.

Map Margins

To make the best use of the space, our fold-out map has no margins. Some weight-conscious backpackers are rumored to cut the margins off all their maps.

But the margins are full of information. Some of the material in the margins of topographic maps fits better into one of the next three chapters. Other information is of little importance for walking, skiing, canoeing, or whatever, but you may want to know what it is all about.

What follows comes from the margins that have been cut from our foldout map.

In the top right corner you'll find the map title:

FALL RIVER PASS QUADRANGLE,
COLORADO
7.5 Minute Series (Topographic)

That uniquely describes this map. Don't omit the name of the state. I don't believe there is another Fall River in another state, but I know of some other quadrangle names duplicated say in North Carolina. At any rate, with more than 2000 maps covering Colorado alone, it would be difficult for the Geological Survey to mail you the right map without knowing the state of the quadrangle.

All quads of the lower 48 states and Hawaii are named for some prominent feature on that sheet, such as a peak, a lake, or a town.

The "7.5 Minute" part of the title becomes clear when you look at the bottom right corner of the map. It's marked 40°22′30″ for North latitude, while the top right corner is labeled 40°30′. The difference is 7′30″, or 7½′. The bottom right and top corners are marked 105°45′ for West longitude, and the left corners read 105°52′30″. The difference is again 7½′. All maps of this series cover 7½′ latitude and 7½′ longitude.

The title is repeated in slightly altered form in the bottom right corner:

FALL RIVER PASS, COLO
N4022.5-W10545 / 7.5

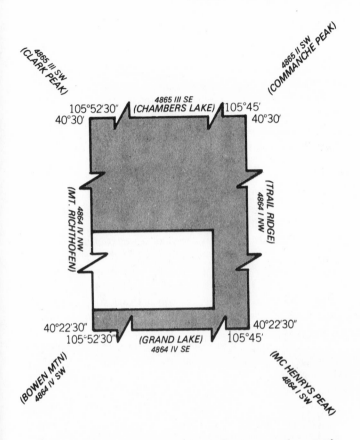

Figure 2.1 *Latitude, longitude, and titles of adjoining maps shown in the margins of the Fall River Pass quad. White area shows the coverage of the fold-out map in the back of this book.*

You'll recognize the abbreviated latitude—latitude by custom is always given first—and longitude from the bottom right corner of the map itself. That's the logical place to start the count of the 7.5' since latitude in this part of the world increases upward, longitude toward the left. Both these directions are easily memorized— they are exactly opposite to the way we write.

In the top left corner of the margin you'll find this credit line:

United States
Department of the Interior
Geological Survey

On some maps, such as those of North Carolina, you may find the Tennessee Valley Authority (TVA), Maps and Surveys Branch credited.

The explanation is in the bottom left corner. The vast majority of U.S. topo quads carry this notice:

Mapped, edited and published by the Geological Survey

On the TVA maps the notice reads: "Mapped and edited by the Tennessee Valley Authority."

Underneath that you often find another statement: "Control by USGS [that's our friends the Geological Survey] and USC&GS [Coast and Geodetic Survey, now NOS/NOAA—National Ocean Survey/National Oceanic and Atmospheric Administration]," meaning that both agencies provided vertical and horizontal ground controls.

Modern maps also carry the statement "Topography from aerial photographs by photogrammetric methods." That refers to the stereo method described earlier. Our map's aerial photographs were taken in 1953 and field checked in 1958. We had to use this map until 1977.

That's not as bad as it sounds. The important topography will not have changed. Roads may have improved or gone to pot. There may have been new trails built (not very likely), and others may have almost disappeared for lack of upkeep.

National Park ranger offices here and National Forest offices elsewhere are a good source of information on trails. They issue maps that are not nearly as useful for topography but that show every trail and fire road in the area. By all means get one. The map will show numbers for the footways and jeep rails. The numbers are likely to be posted at each trailhead, which makes land navigation easy.

A purple notice in the margin of our map shows that the map was revised from aerial photographs taken in 1976 that were not field checked.

The legend at the bottom of the map will continue: "Polyconic projection, 1927 North American datum." The first part describes the method by which the approximately spherical earth has been translated onto the flat sheet of the map. The datum is the surveyor's initial point used as the basic reference point for maps of the United States, Canada, Mexico, and Central American countries. (It is located on the Meades Ranch in central Kansas, west and a little south of Waldo, which you may find on a map on Route 281 not far north of I-70.)

Then come some notes, of interest mostly to mapmakers, that tie the specific map into a larger system of maps. On our map they read: "10,000-foot grid based on Colorado coordinate system, north zone. 1000-meter Universal Transverse Mercator grid ticks, zone 13, shown in blue."

Another line states that this map complies with National Map Accuracy Standards. That's the accuracy you read about earlier.

Some maps, including ours, show a key to road classification.

Ah yes, and then there is a commercial: "For sale by U.S. Geological Survey, Box 25268, Federal Center, Denver, Colorado 80225."

And a free bonus: "A folder describing topographic maps and symbols is available on request." Get it by all means.

Map Symbols

The master key to colors on topographic maps, reduced to its simplest applications, is green for woodlands, brown for contours, blue for water, red for roads and survey lines, and black for man-made objects including names. You can see all these uses on our map.

Of course there are finer points. No one map is likely to show all the possible map symbols. (You are not likely to find tropical mangroves, a glacier, and an urban area close together.)

Symbols Printed in Black

Some of the symbols printed in black ink don't require any study. If you saw the mast of a ship and part of its hull sticking out at an odd angle from some blue area, you'd read that for a wreck.

Other symbols are labeled or can be interpreted easily. For example, broken black lines mark boundaries. Different weights of line and length of dashes are used for national, state, county, and other boundaries. One boundary runs across our map, the Continental Divide. No question there. Elsewhere you might find a broken line with the label Colorado on one side of it and Utah on the other. Again, no need to memorize the line code.

You already know that little black squares or T- or L-shapes indicate dwellings. (Black shading indicates places of business, warehouses, and so on.) The only remnants on our map are two buildings straddling the red squares numbered 7 and 12. (When I selected this particular map there was a cluster of buildings there, and more buildings elsewhere on the map. The two survivors of the 1977 photorevision were part of the Phantom Valley Ranch.)

A black square with a pennant means a school; with a cross it means a church. A cross inside a dashed enclosure indicates a cemetery. If it's large enough you'll find the letters "Cem" inside the enclosure.

There are no railroads on our map. But if you saw a black line with little crossties you'd figure out its meaning.

Telephone lines, pipelines, and so on—black dashed lines—are always labeled. Power lines are dashed lines with large dots symbolizing the supports; metal towers are shown as tiny squares at the exact location.

For many readers the most interesting black lines are the dashed trail lines. Several labeled trails are on our map; for example, the Red Mountain trail near the bottom left corner.

It starts near the two houses, where it runs into two parallel lines that indicate some kind of a (rather poor) road. According to the key printed on the map itself (but cut off in our sample), it's a light-duty road with a hard or improved surface. Had the road been unimproved, say a forest fire road, it would be shown by two interrupted lines, like a string of equal signs.

X-marks and triangles with a dot in the center, with or without the letters BM or VABM, give the exact point where the elevation printed next to it has been measured. These are discussed in Chapter 4.

If you can recognize the symbols shown in Figure 2.2, you know all the ones you are likely to encounter printed in black.

And don't forget the landmark symbol—a circle with a dot in the center. The dot gives the exact location of almost anything. Some of the labels used are more obvious than others. A few useful examples: TR for tower, hence R TR for radio tower, TV TR for television tower; FS and FP for flagstaff or flagpole; CHY for chimney; MON for monument.

Symbols Printed in Color

Red is used for hard surface roads; solid for primary highways, interrupted—as on our map—for secondary highways. If you saw a fat red line with a black line through the center you could probably figure it out: divided highway. When the dividing strip is more than 25 feet (8 meters) wide, the two red lines are separated.

Red is also used for survey lines, like the rectangles and squares on our map, and for fence and field lines. A red tint (see the symbols in color printed alongside our map) is used to show a built-up area where streets and buildings are omitted.

All water features are printed in blue. So are permanent snowfields and glaciers.

Our map shows many ponds and several lakes and streams. All of the streams are less than 25 feet wide, hence are shown as single blue lines.

That includes the mighty Colorado, which runs south past the two buildings on our map. If the river were more than 25 feet wide, the map would show its banks with blue in between.

But here you are very close to the source of the Colorado River. Less than a mile north of the top of our

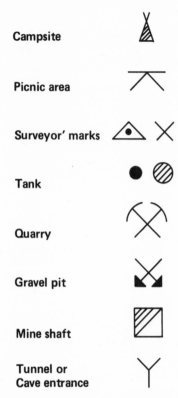

Campsite	
Picnic area	
Surveyor' marks	
Tank	
Quarry	
Gravel pit	
Mine shaft	
Tunnel or Cave entrance	

Figure 2.2 *Map symbols always printed in black. For colored symbols, see the fold-out map in the back of this book.*

map, the trail, which started out as the Colorado River trail and became the La Poudre Pass trail, crosses the Colorado. When I last crossed it, there was a plank to walk on. But even with a fully loaded backpack you could have jumped across it.

The Grand Ditch, near the left margin of our map, obviously is also less than 25 feet wide. The word *grand* does not refer to size or the marvel of it but to the earlier name of the Colorado, Grand River, as in Grand Lake.

The Grand Ditch, with the service road alongside it, was built mostly with pick and shovel at the turn of the century. Its purpose: to bring rainfall and snowmelt from the west slope of the Never Summer Mountains to the arid eastern side of the Continental Divide. It still does.

You won't have much trouble reading or remembering the other map symbols printed in blue.

One warning: when you are canoeing or kayaking, don't trust the rapids and falls symbols on the map. They are easily overlooked, the mapmaker's small falls may turn out to be Class V, and a thrilling ride at one water level can become a death trap at another. Get local information—not from the friendly storekeeper, but from someone who's come down today.

You'll read a lot more about contours, printed in brown, in Chapter 4.

The symbols for cut and fill are tricky. You have to look very closely, and you'll understand them only if you recognize depression contours—contours with little barbs pointing downhill.

The best way I know to get familiar with maps and map symbols is to use them. Perhaps you could get a topo map of your neighborhood or some area you know well and take mental walks, recognizing on the map many of the familiar landmarks. Better yet, if you can, take a real walk with the map in hand.

The symbols used on U.S. topographic maps are also used on other U.S. maps, including those of lakes and rivers and the coastlines of nautical charts. Virtually the same symbols are used on maps of Canada and on official maps of the rest of the world.

If you hike abroad, say in the European Alps, you'll find some of the most useful maps are not published by government agencies but by private interests. The maps of the Austrian Alpine Club—some available with or without ski routes—and the widely sold Kompass Wanderkarten series are good examples. They are based on government maps but have been redrawn to keep one group of mountains together on one sheet. Government maps split such areas along lines of latitude and longitude.

Both sets of maps mentioned above use red for trails rather than roads. (Roads are shown in yellow.) Different symbols are used for well-marked (and numbered) trails, less well-marked trails, and trails that in spots require technical skills. These and all other symbols not in the international code are decoded on the map itself. Kompass gives the legend in German, English, and French.

On the back of many Kompass maps you'll find suggested trips, lists of huts in the area, accommodations in the valley, and so on. You don't have to be fluent in German to get the drift.

Getting the Maps

Perhaps your mountain shop sells topo maps besides sleeping bags and boots and hundreds of other things, but it's not the best source for maps. A shop in Maine isn't likely to stock maps of Colorado, and vice versa.

The maps that interest us most—the 7½ × 7½ and 15 × 15 minute hiking maps—in 1988 list for $2.50 per map direct from the government. Postage is $1 per order. On orders of $10 or more the postage is included. The ½ × 1 and 1 × 2 degree planning maps cost $4 each with postage as for the hiking maps.

To get any discount a dealer has to order and pay in advance for at least 200 maps. That's not very profitable business; so you can expect to pay a dealer a dollar or two above the direct-from-the-government price per map.

Even though that may not bankrupt you, it'll deprive you of the fun of planning your map selection months before you actually get away.

Let's pretend you start from scratch.

The first step is to write for the free Index of Topographic maps of the state where you plan to hike. Theoretically, only one index map is sent without charge, but in my experience they honor reasonable requests—say for two or three adjoining states. Just don't expect to paper your basement at the taxpayers' expense by ordering index maps of all fifty states. If you forget to mention the state you want, they'll send you the index for the state where you live.

In the same letter also request the free pamphlet Topographic Map Symbols.

For requesting *index* maps of all the United States and possessions the address is National Cartographic Information Center, 507 National Center, Reston, VA 22092.

For ordering *all other* maps write to the Branch of Distribution, U.S. Geological Survey, Box 25268, Federal Center, Denver, CO 80225.

If you live in Alaska, you'll save time by requesting indexes directly from the Distribution Section, U.S.

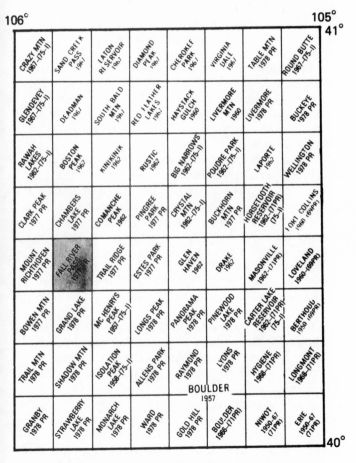

Figure 2.3 *Part of Colorado index sheet.*

Geological Survey, Federal Building, Box 12, 101 12th Avenue, Fairbanks, Alaska 99701.

A brown 9-by-12-inch (24-by-32-centimeter) envelope will bring your index, which unfolds into a map about 2 by 3 feet (60 by 90 centimeters), and an order form.

The main map shows the outline of the state covered with little rectangles. Most of them will have the quadrangle name (and year of issue) printed diagonally. These are our 7½′ quads.

A few quadrangles, four times larger than these quads, with the name printed horizontally, stand for 15′ topo maps.

You may think you'd save a lot of money by buying quads that cover the larger area yet cost no more. Unfortunately, you lose some detail that way. Also, for many areas there are no 15′ topo maps. Relatively few areas give you no choice the other way, where 7½′ maps have not yet been published.

Alaska is an exception to this. There are only a few 7½′ quads available. Also, in place of names the quads carry designations such as A1, B1, and so on within a larger map area that is named, such as Fairbanks. You must give both the name of the larger area and the letter and number when you are ordering a map; for example, Fairbanks A1.

Caution: occasionally a 7½′ and a 15′ map may have the same name. For example, the 7½′ Boulder quad covers the Southeast quarter of the 15′ Boulder map. Be precise when writing your order.

On a separate drawing on the same side of the index sheet you'll find outlines of some other topographic maps, which you'll read about in the next chapter. I suggest you hold off getting maps until you have read about them.

On the opposite side of the index sheet you'll find a list of libraries that have a collection of topographic maps of the state, such as the Denver Public Library. If you happen to be in Denver, that would be a fine place to look at the index and then at some 7½′ and 15′ maps to see if you really need them for your proposed trip. College and university libraries may let you consult their collections if you ask the right way.

The first map for every trip is the hardest to locate on the index map. A random search won't do; there are more than 2000 quads shown on the Colorado index, for example.

A map of the state is the place to start. Get the approximate latitude (from left or right margin) and longitude (from top or bottom) of the area where you want to go. Then look for the corresponding figures on the index map, remembering that the figures increase upward and toward the left. (One degree equals 60', which makes 15' one-quarter and 7½' one-eighth of a degree.) Often a familiar name, say Estes Park, will jump out at you when you are anywhere near the right spot.

One map will lead you to others. Every topo map, as you have seen, has the names of the eight adjoining quads printed in the margins and corners (see Figure 2.1).

Next comes a list of dealers that sell the state's maps. It includes places you would never have tried on your own, such as bookstores, blueprint shops, and motels. It doesn't include some National Park and National Forest offices that stock maps of their own area as a convenience for their visitors.

Besides maps of the United States and the whole state, this side of the sheet also lists special maps and their prices. By all means glance at that list. You may find a very useful map there. For example, the Colorado index lists Rocky Mountain National Park, which includes the Fall River Pass 7.5' quadrangle and shows at a glance what other quads you need to cover the entire park on that scale.

When you start your want list you'll make a discovery that everybody has made at least once: it takes more maps than you thought.

In Colorado a 7½' map covers an area of about 8½ by 6½ miles (10 by 14 kilometers). Yet a 6-mile (10-kilometer) hike always seems to take two and sometimes three maps.

If you are interested in topo maps of Canada, write for the free Index of National Topographic System Maps to the Canada Map Office, 615 Booth Street, Ottawa, Ontario, Canada K1A OE9.

Each Canadian index is a large map as in the U.S. system. Index 1 covers the Maritime Provinces, Quebec, and Ontario; index 2 covers Manitoba and the western provinces; and index 3 covers the Northwest Territories.

Folding and Protecting Maps

I suggested that you hold off ordering or buying maps for a trip until you have read the next chapter. But this seems the right place to discuss storing and mounting maps and such housekeeping chores.

Maps are sold and usually mailed flat—that is, unfolded and rolled.

Land navigators don't share the superstition of mariners that outlaws folding. On the trail you may occa-

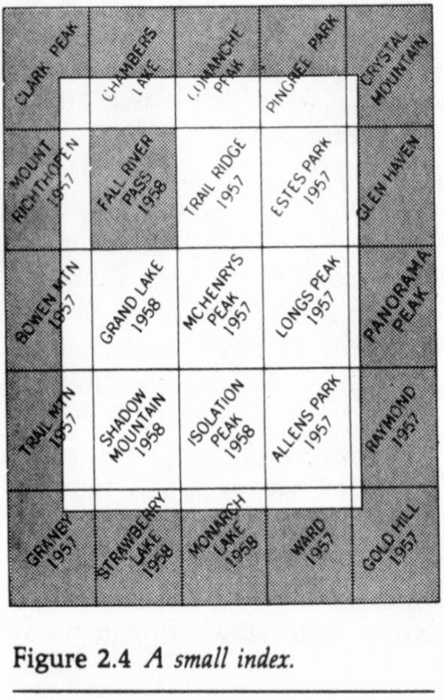

Figure 2.4 *A small index.*

sionally see a map rolled around a fishing rod case. But I find a rolled map outdoors a pain.

Some maps come folded to pocket size—for example, the 1:100,000 topographic maps discussed in the next chapter; here "pocket size" means about the size of the page you are reading. The Kompass maps are about the same size, the Alpine Club maps a bit larger, 5 by 8 inches (14 by 22 centimeters). Both come in sturdy plastic pockets.

Before you start folding maps every which way, let me jump ahead a bit.

With the type of compass that is most popular now, it is useful to have one of the vertical margins of the folded map accessible on whatever part of the map you may be working.

One way to achieve that is to fold the maps vertically in half, printed side out. It does not matter how you fold them horizontally. I'd fold the 15' map in half, but the larger 7½' is a bit awkward that way. I'd fold it in thirds. That way both maps end up about 9 by 11 inches (23 by 28 centimeters).

Unfortunately that's larger than the map pockets on many backpacks. They need the 7½' map folded three times each way. So you end up with nine sections, three of which have no printed vertical margins.

You can overcome that shortcoming by making the vertical folds carefully. You don't have to measure anything. Top and bottom margins are already divided in three sections that are each 2½' wide. On the map from which ours was cut, they are marked 47'30" and 50'. To make your task easier the map shows crosses one-third and two-thirds of the way up. You'll see one cross near the middle of our map, near Squeak Creek; another at the same distance from the bottom near the right margin.

Some people mount their maps on canvas; others laminate them. It all sounds great and certainly makes the map last longer. But it's a lot of work and impossible to do when you pick up a map at the local hardware store on the way to the trailhead. The economics seem all wrong to me too. Not counting your time, you pay out more than a new—and possibly updated—map would cost.

There are some nifty map cases with transparent windows on the market. One type has grommets that let you string a lanyard to carry the map dangling from your neck.

Your neck gets a lot of wear in outdoor sports. You should carry your compass (and perhaps an altimeter) around it. Some people suggest you carry a whistle (to let the rest of your party know they've lost you). Many of us carry a camera. And all this in addition to your medical tag that tells rescuers you are allergic to Hungarian goulash.

The simplest and cheapest map case is a gallon-size Ziploc bag that just about fits a 15' map folded in four, or a 7½' map folded in six sections. Trimming one white border of the map a bit lets you zip up the bag. When one bag gets too ratty for map use, you can demote it to refuse bag and take a new one.

3.
Distance from the Map

We have agreed that maps show land areas greatly reduced in size. But how much reduced?

That'll depend on how large a land area the map shows and, much less, on the size of the map; much less, because map sizes don't differ as much as the areas to be mapped.

The map that used to hang in your schoolroom was perhaps eight feet wide; the double page map in this book is about as many inches wide. They differ by a factor of 12.

The world is in very round figures 25,000 miles (40,000 kilometers) around the equator; New York City is about 20 miles (32 kilometers) wide from East to West. If you wanted to map both, and used the same reduction, the map of the world would have to be 1250 times wider than the one of New York, which is obviously impractical. The major thoroughfares of New York City could be reasonably well shown on a double page of this book. The same rate of reduction would make a map of the world almost as wide as the lengths of three football fields.

You have lived with maps of about the same size—folded road maps, or maps in a road atlas, for instance—all your life. Such maps must have different rates of reduction, or to use a shorter term, different *scales*.

You may have planned a trip to the West Coast on a map of the United States showing only the major highways and cities. For side trips, or as you approached your destination, for more detailed information you would have used a map that showed only California, or perhaps only southern California. Then, to find the best approach to your aunt's place in Redondo Beach, you should have switched—or wished you had switched—to a map of Los Angeles.

To show the roughly 3000 miles (about 4800 kilometers) from coast to coast, the publishers of your road atlas shrank the distance by a factor of 9,000,000 to about 21 inches (53 centimeters). The scale of that map would be described as 1:9,000,000.

That scale makes 1 inch on the map equal to 9,000,000 inches in the landscape (about 142 statute miles). It makes 1 centimeter on the map equal to 9,000,000 centimeters in the landscape (exactly 90 kilometers).

On the trip to the West Coast, when you saw the mountains you had to take a side trip. Perhaps to the less used western part of Rocky Mountain National Park. On the map of the United States you can barely find the park. So you switch to a map of Colorado.

On that map the 77 almost straight miles from Burlington (near the Kansas border) to Limon (where the road to Colorado Springs peels off) measure about three and a half inches. The scale works out to 1:1,400,000.

The map of Greater Los Angeles, which shows most through streets, is drawn on a scale of 1:300,000. (One mile equals about ¼ inch; one kilometer, about 3 millimeters.)

Many people get confused when they hear or read about small-scale or large-scale maps.

A small-scale map shows a large area (such as the United States) with little detail—showing large features only; the figure following the 1: is large (for example, 9,000,000).

Obviously, each of the above statements is the other way around on a large-scale map. This may help you remember the facts:

Small-scale map	*Large-scale map*
Number after 1: *large*	Number after 1: *small*
Area covered *large*	Area covered *small*
Large features only	*Small* features shown

If life has taught you that things often are the reverse of what you expected, that's the way to remember it.

Mathematically inclined readers will have already realized that the scale of a map can be just as easily expressed as a fraction: 1/9,000,000, 1/300,000, and so on.

For hiking, skiing, canoeing, and other activities that take us perhaps as far in one day as an automobile might take us in a quarter hour or less, we need maps on much larger scales than even the Greater Los Angeles map.

You already know that we'd use topographic maps for these activities, maps that show the ups and downs of the terrain by contour lines. Such maps in the United States are mainly on two pairs of slightly different scales.

For maximum detail, the generally available largest scale is either 1:24,000 or 1:25,000. That makes 1 inch exactly equal to 2000 feet, the scale of the most popular 7½' topo quads of the contiguous states.

Metric countries unimpeded by miles and inches have no reason to use that scale. They use 1:25,000, which makes one kilometer equal to exactly 40 millimeters. You'll find this scale used on Canadian maps, on the Austrian Alpine Club maps, and also on maps of Alaska. The detail and the area that can be shown on a given sheet size are, of course, virtually the same with these two scales. Eventually all U.S. maps in the 7½' series will use the 1:25,000 scale.

The second set of scales used on U.S. topographic maps is 1:62,500 and 1:63,360. A statute mile equals exactly 5280 feet, or 63,360 inches. On a map on the scale of 1:63,360, one mile equals exactly one inch. That is the scale of most topographic quads in Alaska.

The rest of the United States uses the scale of 1:62,500, so that one mile for our purposes is still one inch, for the 15′ topo quads.

But why that scale? Simply because it is exactly four times larger than the 1:250,000 scale used on another series of topographic maps.

Countries on the metric system don't have any interest in statute miles and so use neither of these scales. Their nearest equivalent is 1:50,000, one-half the 1:25,000 scale, making one kilometer exactly 20 millimeters on the map. You'll run across that scale on European hiking maps and Canadian topo maps.

The scale of 1:250,000 mentioned above is used on another series of topographic maps and is tied to an international reference system; each map covers one degree of latitude and two degrees of longitude (three degrees in Alaska). On that scale a mile becomes ¼ inch (6 millimeters), which is too small for actual hiking but a good size for planning your approach or an extended trip that would spill over several larger-scale sheets. It's also a useful map for identifying distant mountains, lakes, and settlements that are well off your actual hiking map. Such distant landmarks can sometimes help you find out where you are.

You may like the 1:100,000 series topo maps even better for such uses. They cover only one-quarter the area of the 1:250,000 maps—30′ latitude by 1° longitude. But a mile becomes a more useful ⅝ inch (16 millimeters), and these maps are much better suited for getting your location from distant mapped features. It also makes an emergency hiking map, say for an area you hadn't planned to visit. And it's a good scale for bicycle touring. Unfortunately these maps are not available for many areas (unlike the 1:250,000 series maps). Colorado, for example, would need 56 of these maps; only 10 have been published.

The price for both the 1:100,000 and 1:25,000 series maps is currently $2 postpaid.

Summary of Map Series

A good way to visualize all the different U.S. topographic maps would be to superimpose samples of each series on the map of a state. Let's use Colorado, not only because our map is from that state, but because Colorado has such a nice regular shape. It reaches from latitude 37°N to 41°N, and from longitude 102°03'W to 109°03'W. That's exactly 4° latitude by 7° longitude.

Each of the large quadrangles (1° latitude and 2° longitude) in Figure 3.1 shows one of the state's topographic maps on the scale of 1:250,000. It takes, as you can see or calculate, 16 of these maps to cover the state of Colorado, with half of each of the 4 westernmost maps overlapping into Utah. All these quadrangles are available.

The smaller quadrangle at the top, labeled Craig, is one of the few 1:100,000 quadrangles covering ½° latitude by 1° longitude (or 30' latitude by 60' longitude if you prefer to think that way to compare with the next

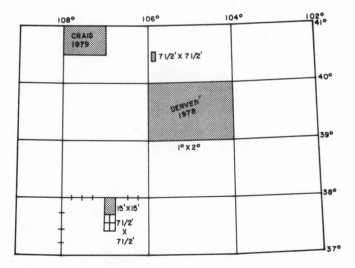

Figure 3.1 *Topo map areas.*

maps). Few such quadrangles have so far been published.

The next smaller size quadrangles represent the 15'-by-15' 1:62,500 topographic maps. You can see that it would take 32 of these maps to cover the area of one 1:250,000 scale map. (In Alaska these quadrangles cover uniformly 15' latitude, but vary in coverage of longitude from 20' to 36'.) The coverage of the state by these quadrangles is far from total.

The smallest quadrangles represent the popular 7½'-by-7½' topo maps on the 1:24,000 scale. (In Puerto Rico the scale would be 1:20,000.) The one near the top of Figure 3.1 shows the relation in size to the 1:250,000 scale maps. It takes 128 of the larger-scale maps to cover the area of the smaller-scale map. The small quadrangles at the lower left of the figure show the relation of the 7½'-by-7½' maps to the 15'-by-15'. It takes four 1:24,000 topo quads to cover the same area as one of the 1:62,500 maps.

This is the most detailed series available. The vast majority of the quads needed to cover the state of Colorado (1792 in all) are actually available. Where there are gaps, the 15'-by-15' quads fill in.

Don't let Figure 3.1 and what you just read mislead you into thinking that the map covering the largest area is large and the one covering the smallest area is small. All four maps in the different series are rather similar in size. (Actually the 30'-by-60' map is the largest, the 15'-by-15' map the smallest.)

The similarity of size is no accident. A 5-foot-wide map is a nuisance to handle on a desk; on a mountain it would threaten to kite off, taking you with it.

Measuring Distances

Maps let you find the distance between any two mapped points, usually more accurately than any of us will ever need it.

Anybody can learn in a few minutes how to measure distances on maps accurately. But one-tenth of a mile or a kilometer hardly ever matters. To my mind, what matters is that you hardly ever make a

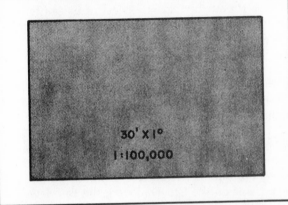

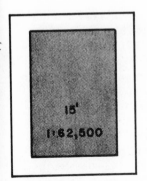

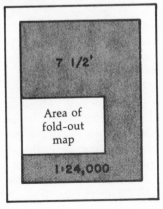

Figure 3.2 *Relative sizes of topo maps.*

gross mistake, and when you do that you notice it before your party has to sleep on scree and cook with dew.

The way to avoid mistakes, or to catch them, is to get a feel for the scale of the map you are using. That's not difficult. You probably use only one scale on any one day—say, a 15' series topo map. You may have become hypnotized by all the dull figures about scales in the last few pages and have forgotten that on these maps one mile is almost exactly one inch.

If you were raised an inch at a time, that's all you need. After measuring a distance on the map, say 5½ miles, think: "Does that look like 5½ inches?"

If it does, it probably is right. Most of us can tell 5½ inches from 4½ or 6½ inches; or at least get suspicious enough to double-check.

If you grew up a centimeter at a time and think of distances in kilometers, you'd have to remember that on the 15' maps 16 millimeters represent one kilometer. You'd know you had goofed if you measured what looks like much more or much less than 9 centimeters.

Test yourself. On our map one mile is 2⅝ inches (2½ inches is close enough), and one kilometer is 42 millimeters (40 millimeters is close enough).

How far is it on the Ute Trail from the Fairview Curve (bottom of the map, near the center) to Milner Pass? Just looking at it, wouldn't you say about two miles (or three kilometers)?

You can get the necessary base numbers for miles or kilometers in inches or millimeters from Table 3.1. You'll see from the table that on 1:100,000 maps 1 kilometer is exactly 1 centimeter. That's easily remembered, and not just because it's simple. It has to be so: 1 kilometer equals 1000 meters, and 1 meter equals 100 centimeters. So 1 centimeter times 100,000—the scale of the map—equals 1 kilometer.

All other metric equivalents come easy after that: 1:50,000 means 2 centimeters per kilometer, 1:25,000 means 4 centimeters, 1:250,000 works out to 4 millimeters, and so on.

Table 3.1 Distance equivalents for commonly used scales*

Scale	Maps	1 statute mile equals about: Inches	1 statute mile equals about: Millimeters	1 kilometer equals about: Inches	1 kilometer equals about: Millimeters
Hiking Maps					
1:20,000	Puerto Rico 7½'	3⅛	80	2	50†
1:24,000	**7½' quads**	**2⅝**	**67**	**1⅝**	**42**
1:25,000	Metric maps	2½	64	1⅝	40†
1:50,000	Metric maps	1¼	32	¾	20†
1:62,500	**15' quads**	**1**	**26**	**⅝**	**16**
1:63,360	Alaska 15'	1†	25	⅝	16
Planning Maps					
1:100,000	U.S., metric	⅝	16	⅜	10†
1:250,000	U.S., metric	¼	6½	5⁄32	4†

*The most commonly used U.S. maps are in boldface type.
†Exactly.

I'm not suggesting you should eyeball distances. Just check your measurements that way.

To help with measurements, the U.S. maps discussed have graphic scales in both American standard and metric units. Foreign maps may have only metric units. Then you have a choice: you can quickly learn to live with kilometers, as some travelers adapt to the local beer price in local currency; or you can convert as other travelers do. A kilometer is about six tenths (actually 0.621) statute mile. One mile is about 1.6 (actually 1.609) kilometers.

Using metric 1:25,000 scale maps will seem very simple if you are used to the 7½' series, which is on the scale of 1:24,000. The two scales are identical as far as hiking or skiing is concerned. The difference is only 4 percent of the distance.

Basic Measuring Techniques

How can you bring the distance between two points down to the scale at the bottom of the map?

There are several solutions.

One is to take a match box, matchfolder, twig, or match and measure that. You may find that your matchfolder is by chance exactly two miles on the 15' map you are using. Then you can step off two miles in any direction you like, even around corners.

Or try this. Say the problem is to find the distance from where you left your car near the buildings straddling squares 7 and 12 to where the Red Mountain trail joins the road along the Grand Ditch. I'd break a match, or a pine needle, so it's ½ mile long on the scale. I'd then weasel it around all the corners of the trail and get six times and a bit. The distance is therefore about 3 miles plus, or call it 3¼ miles.

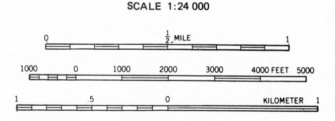

SCALE 1:24 000

SCALE 1:62 500

Figure 3.3 *Graphic scales.*

I usually carry pipe cleaners in my breast pocket. They are handy for many purposes—tying bags, as a zipper tab extension, even for cleaning a pipe. They also make good map-measuring instruments. Most are 6 inches (15 centimeters) long, but you can buy longer ones.

I put my pipe cleaner on the graphic scale and bend it sharply at the two-mile mark on a 7½' quad, or at the five-mile mark on a 15' quad.

To solve the Red Mountain trail problem, I'd start my pipe cleaner at either end of the trail, then bend it to make all the turns as closely as possible. The pipe cleaner may tend to straighten out by itself. I don't worry about the part that has already been measured, and just keep a finger on the last spot to keep it in place. I'd make the distance one 2-mile pipecleaner plus a piece that measured 1.1 miles when held against the scale. Call it 3⅛ miles in all.

Crude? Perhaps.

Maybe you know of a gadget that you wheel over the map and that magically adds up all the distances you have pushed it. Sooner or later someone who's heard you are "into maps" will give you one. My advice: trade it in for granola bars. These gadgets work fine on a chart table. On a map that has been folded and now is balanced on your left knee they'll be no more accurate than my match or pipe cleaner, which are lighter and no great loss when they disappear.

But there are two tools that come in handy in map work. Both are quite inexpensive.

The first is a dime store ruler. If you can, get a transparent one that lets you see the map under it. They come in 6- and 12-inch (15- and 30-centimeter) lengths; I prefer the longer ones.

We'll find uses in compass work for such a ruler. It's well worth the price—currently 29 cents and up—and adds less than an ounce (30 grams) to your load. (It also makes a great back scratcher if you're hiking by yourself.)

People who—when they are not paddling, hiking, biking, or whatever—design or make things to thousandths of an inch, weigh in milligrams, and balance books to the penny are likely to be appalled at my pipe cleaner measuring technique. You'd better not get your hopes up that a ruler will put some precision into your navigation.

I might excuse approximate measurements by arguing that a mile in the mountains isn't a mile anyway. I'm not even talking about "uphill miles" that seem longer and steeper the heavier the canoe you're portaging or the heavier your backpack.

Even a level mile on a high plateau is longer than in flat land near sea level. Every point is mapped where a plumb line would touch the sea level below it. It has to be.

Imagine an island rising out of the sea with perpendicular cliffs and a flat top. The high land is part of a larger sphere than the sea is part of, and a mile measured on top of the island would be longer than a sea-level tunnel below it that measured exactly a mile.

That's absolutely correct and may win you a bet when you are snowed in someday and can't find anything else to argue about. But it's totally irrelevant to our navigation. If the island were a mile (about 1600 meters) high, the clifftop mile would measure 16 inches (41 centimeters) more than the sea-level mile.

Far more significant is the difference between slope length and the distance measured or mapped on the flat. The Ute Trail, for example, climbs rather gently from the Fairview Curve to Milner Pass. (You'd probably drive the section of Trail Ridge Road that parallels it in high gear.) The difference between mapped distance and actual trail distance is only 18 feet (5½ meters). But instead of taking Red Mountain trail to the Grand Ditch, let's scramble up in imagination by the shortest route, about 6/10 mile (1 kilometer) long. Smoothing out the varying grades of that route, you'd find it 220 feet (67 meters) longer than the mapped distance. That's still not much—about 7 percent. On the steepest part of that scramble, a real grunt, the difference between actual and mapped distances becomes 19 percent.

Next time you're snowed in, turn the conversation to real estate. If you're lucky someone is going to talk about land swindles. Say someone, though warned by everybody, bought one acre (about 4000 square meters) of land in Colorado, sight unseen. When he did see it, it turned out to be dry, roadless, billygoat land—worthless. The developer, of course, had left without leaving a forwarding address.

Ah, but there is a consolation. If the land was as steep as the steepest part of the Red Mountain short-cut, the buyer really owned one acre plus a good-sized lot, about 100 by 83 feet (770 square meters).

But back to the ruler.

It isn't often that we deal with straight-line distances, but when we do, rulers are an easy way to pick them off the map proper and carry them to the graphic scale of your choice (miles, feet, kilometers).

You may be opposed to the metric system, for whatever reason. But there is a way of taking advantage of the metric edge of the ruler without adopting the metric system, or what scientifically is called the Système International. Unless from cabinetmaking or some other hobby or profession you are very sure and quick in readings of sixteenths and thirty-secondths of an inch, you'll find this method faster and less error-prone.

The numbers 1 to 30 on the 12-inch rule indicate centimeters. But you don't care about that. Each centimeter is divided into ten parts. For easy reading every fifth unit—we might as well call them millimeters, although you don't have to—is marked by a longer line.

That makes counting the small divisions easy. They run from 0 at the lower numeral through 1, 2, 3, and 4 to the longer mark; then come 6, 7, 8, and finally 9 just before the next higher numeral.

I think few people strictly count marks. Without

Figure 3.4 *Metric marks on a ruler.*

much thought they call the mark to the left of the longer mark 4; to the right 6; to the left of the next numeral 9; and so on.

You can suit yourself about what to call the result
of your measurement. You could call it 5.4 or 5.6 (with
or without adding "centimeters"). Or perhaps 54, 56,
and 58 (with or without "millimeters" added.)

Transfer the marks to the graphic scales, say the
miles scale. On a 1:24,000 map your 54 whatevers will
measure 8/10 mile.

You don't have to read the metric scale at all if you
don't want to; just keep the nail of your index finger
(or thumb) on the mark when you move the ruler to
the scale.

A twig picked up on the spot could be used in the
same way. But for compass work it won't do. You'll
soon see why.

The second handy map tool is a magnifier. Nothing
elaborate is needed, but a magnifier at times is a great
help in, say, counting contour lines. Sometimes a
pocket magnifier can save you digging out your reading
glasses, exchanging them for the sunglasses you were
wearing, and reversing the whole process.

You may want to test yourself. Where the Red
Mountain Trail meets the Grand Ditch, near the little
pond, do you see from left to right a thin brown line,
the blue of the ditch, two parallel black lines (the
road), the dashes marking the trail, and a heavier
brown line?

Many modern compasses have a magnifier molded
into the base. Held a little distance from the map, it'll
do the trick. Even if your compass is so equipped, you
may want to carry a magnifier for observing the details
of flowers or butterflies.

Here's another method of getting trail distances on a
mapped trail even if the graphic scale isn't showing
and you are out of pipe cleaners, matches, and pine
needles. It's such a simple method—I don't know why
I didn't think of it before Mr. Kroether put it into *Backpacker Footnotes*.

First, find a straight section of a trail on your map.

On it measure ½ mile (or ½ kilometer, depending on your persuasion). Then count the dashes in that stretch. (Your magnifier may help.)

Say you get 18 dashes to the ½ mile. Even if the section of trail is not straight—when is it?—if you count 72 dashes between two points, they are about 2 miles apart.

Sections and Section Numbers

If you carry your maps folded, their graphic scales will often be covered or awkward to reach for transferring measurements. But you may have perfectly good scales on the exposed part of the map.

Many topo maps and most forest maps show mysterious squares: land sections as originally surveyed. Each was intended to be as close to 640 acres as possible; that is, one mile by one mile.

On our map the quadrangles labeled 7 and 12 are good examples; so are numbers 18 and 13 on the complete map. Numbers 6 and 1 are rare exceptions, odd-sized sections. (I have not researched what caused these oddities. It could have been a mistake of the original surveyor. If you had bought the section that includes Shipler Mountain, or Hitchens Creek, you would have got more than 900 acres—and nothing can change the original survey. More likely the two odd sections were intended to link up without a gap with two sections just north of them, surveyed earlier for Lulu City. That city, alas, is now only a number of overgrown foundations.)

You can see what a handy scale these squares and the widths of sections 1 and 6 provide. With ruler, pipecleaner, pine needle, or just fingers you can transfer one-mile distances to any part of the map without turning it over or unfolding it.

On 15′ quads and forest maps your whole day's hike may be covered by section lines. If your route happens to be East-West or North-South, all you have to do is count squares and add fractions at each end of the trek, and you have your distance in miles.

If your route should cross the sections diagonally,

say from NE to SW, it helps to know that the diagonal of each square is about 1.4 miles. That makes seven sections traversed diagonally 10 miles.

Trails usually don't follow these simple courses. But any skew trail will have to be between the limits of the shortest (1.0 mile) and the longest straight line (1.4 miles) through any one square. For ten squares that might be between 10 and 14 miles. That's close enough

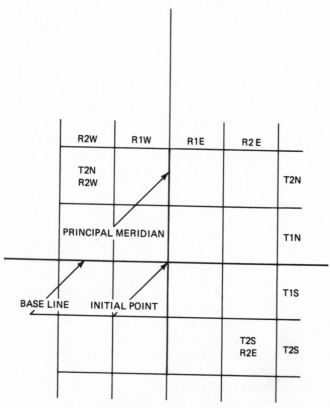

Figure 3.5 *Numbering of townships and ranges.*

for a first guess; 12 miles may be a reasonable estimate for rough planning.

Section Lines

Some readers may have wondered about the numbering of the sections on our map. Why does number 1 border on 6 and 12, for example?

Congress ordered it that way in 1785 upon recommendation of a committee under Mr. Thomas Jefferson.

Somewhat simplified, the scheme is as follows. At a given initial point two lines are established. One, running North-South, is the principal meridian of the area to be surveyed; the other, running East-West, is the base line.

Additional lines are drawn six miles apart and parallel to the principal meridian (range lines). Other lines are drawn also six miles apart but parallel to the base line (township lines). Townships are numbered starting from the base line, both north and south. Ranges are numbered from the principal meridian, both east and west.

That explains the red figures near the top left corner of our map.

The Hitchens Gulch section lies in Township 5 North (T5N), in Range 76 West (R76W). The section containing Shipler Mountain also lies in Township 5 North, but in Range 75 West (R75W).

Each one of the six-by-six mile areas—also often called townships to confuse you—is divided into one-by-one-mile sections, as we already know. The numbering mandated by Congress so long ago starts at

6	5	4	3	2	1
7	8	9	10	11	12
18	17	16	15	14	13
19	20	21	22	23	24
30	29	28	27	26	25
31	32	33	34	35	36

the Northeast corner with 1, going west and snaking
back and forth to end with 36 in the Southeast corner.

That explains the numbering of sections on our map:
1, 12, and 13 are the easternmost sections of R76W; 6,
7, and 18 are the westernmost sections of R75W.

I can almost hear you groan, "So what?"

Someday when you aren't too certain of where you
are—a polite way of saying lost—you may see a yellow
sign with black numbers nailed to a tree. One extra
nail marks the section corner where you are standing.

To the right of the La Poudre Pass Trail, about halfway up our map, the sign would read 5N 76W and the
nail would be at the right edge between the figures 1
and 12.

The numbering scheme is admittedly not the simplest. (Was Mr. Jefferson left-handed?) So many maps
give the numbers of all 36 sections. People who work
with them frequently, surveyors and foresters for example, get familiar enough with them. To keep maps
uncluttered, sometimes only the four corner sections
are numbered, like this:

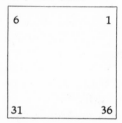

Once you remember the snaking, you can reconstruct
all the other numbers. Your pencil stub may be needed
here.

Section numbers, without any further identification
of township and range, are often a handy way to refer
to a spot on the map. A member of your party may
borrow your map and ask, "Where are we now?" He
knows, of course, that he is trudging up the West Fork.
So the answer "In section 32" is enough; the rest is obvious. That's more elegant than saying "Somewhere
within a finger North of the letter F in Fork."

The four-corner marking scheme is fine for the
1:100,000 maps, but even that would measle the map

with numbers and small squares. So only the
6-by-6-mile squares are printed. That gives you a
quick 6-mile or 10-kilometer scale. The diagonal of
such a square is 8½ statute miles (about 14 kilometers). For the township and range numbers you have to
look at the side and top margins of the map.

Other Techniques

Not surprisingly, the method for finding distance on
most United States topographic maps is somewhat
tilted toward miles.

But there is help for metric users, apart from the
graphic scale in kilometers. On all these maps there are
ticks in all four margins that indicate exactly one kilometer. The absolute distances indicated are of little interest to us; they refer to an international map reference system, called the Universal Tranverse Mercator
(UTM) grid.

Near the right bottom corner of the map that included our map you'd find a mark labeled:

$$_4 \, 35^{000m} \, E$$

The next mark is simply labeled with a small 4 and
a larger 34. What matters is that between these and all
similar marks on other maps, horizontally and vertically, the distance is precisely 1000 meters. There is no
law that says you can't use these marks to give you a
distance of about six-tenths of a statute mile.

Actually the difficulty of switching from American
Standard to metric units is mostly in the user's mind.
You may use 1:100,000 U.S. topographic maps for
planning or identifying distant features of the landscape only to find at the end of the summer that the
map is all metric. You never noticed, because you simply used the graphic miles and feet scales, and perhaps
the section lines.

You are not likely to use a map of that scale for figuring out how steep a trail is. So you never noticed
that the contours were 50 meters apart. A conversion
table on the map itself will tell you the equivalent in
feet (164 feet).

You probably now have enough methods for measuring distance on the maps that interest us to last you forever. But there is one more that's sometimes useful. It works on all maps and globes and needs no graphic scales. You don't even have to know the scale of the map.

The method is based on the fact that 1 minute of latitude, regardless of scale of map or globe, equals 1 nautical mile. You'll find these minutes, as you know, on the left or right margins of a map. (On a globe you'll find them on lines running from the North Pole to the South Pole.) Since there are 60 minutes to a degree, 1 degree of latitude is 60 nautical miles.

Near latitude 45° it is exactly 60 nautical miles. On the equator it is 3/10 mile less, at the poles 3/10 mile more. That's a total error of ½ percent.

I can hear you: "That's bully for sailors, but I don't even remember how long a nautical mile is."

All right. The nautical mile is—close enough for our purposes—15 percent longer than the familiar statute mile. The rule then reads:

> One *minute* of latitude equals
> about 1.15 statute miles.
> One *degree* of latitude equals
> about 69 statute miles.

Don't let me forget the readers who think metrically. For them the easiest way to remember the rule is three ones: one degree of latitude equals about 111 kilometers. (That's no accident. You may recall that during the French Revolution the meter was planned to be the ten millionth part of the distance from equator to the poles. That's 90 degrees. Dividing by 1000 to get kilometers, you get 111 kilometers per degree.)

For minutes of latitude, that does not work as neatly as in English units. One nautical mile, by definition, equals 1852 meters. You could remember:

> One *minute* of latitude equals
> about 1.8 kilometers.
> One *degree* of latitude equals
> about 111 kilometers.

You may want to remember the relation or relations that concern you most. Then you can just glance at a map, even when the numerical scale and the graphic scales are folded under, and announce the distance.

Just imagine the faces of your Austrian friends who are arguing about a distance when you, just glancing at the left margin of a folded Alpenverein's map you have never seen before, announce: "Looks like 9 kilometers to me."

"How does an American know that?"

Answer: it was just about the distance between 20' and 25', which makes it 5 × 1.8 kilometers.

Estimating Travel Time

You may have thought me unforgivably sloppy for giving some very inexact methods for measuring distances on the map. Don't get me wrong. At times, I'm all for the most accurate measurement possible. When I get on a cable car, I fervently hope the engineers measured right and ordered enough cable to reach the top station.

Great accuracy in measuring distances on the map would make sense if we had some way of measuring distance accurately on the trail. But we haven't.

Pedometers that count your paces and can be adjusted to the length of your stride work fine for a disciplined army marching on a road. For free spirits trudging up or sauntering down rocky trails they are not so useful. If you don't believe me, try one on a talus slope.

You may wonder how some guidebooks measured the trail when they say, "After 5.82 miles. . . ." (How do you know when you're there?) Possibly the author used a measuring wheel, a gadget like a map measurer that registers the distance the author has pushed or pulled it. I wonder how accurate that wheel is on some sole-destroying trails. And you certainly wouldn't want to pull or push such a wheel along for your own navigation.

So what it boils down to is this: you get distances

from the map, but what you really want to know is, how long will it take? And later on the trail the question may be, how much longer?

The answer to such questions can be most important.

The weather is just too awful to go on. "How far to where we can turn off and sit it out?" Or early in the afternoon, "Will we make the planned campsite before dark, or should we look for a suitable spot now?"

What we need then is a formula to translate miles (or kilometers) from the map into hours on the trail.

Robert S. Wood in *Pleasure Packing* figures on covering two miles (about three kilometers) per hour on flat or mildly descending trails with a moderate backpacker's load, less than 30 pounds (14 kilograms). For each 1000-foot (300-meter) rise he allows one extra hour. (The next chapter deals with measuring rise, descent, and steepness on the map.)

That formula checks with an old rule of thumb: one to ten. A climb of 100 feet (or meters) equals 1000 feet (or meters) on the flat. Mr. Wood's extra time for 1000 feet equals that for two level miles, not much more than 10,000 feet.

For steeply descending sections of trails he adds one-half hour per 1000 feet (300 meters).

These figures have the beauty of simplicity and are easily remembered. (To keep them simple I have converted to meters with very round figures, for example 300 in place of 328.)

You may find that these delightfully simple figures don't quite fit your style of hiking. Time yourself on a few walks and then adjust the figures (rounded for convenience) to suit your progress.

You may find that with your usual pack weight, taking photographs, admiring the scenery, and retying your shoelaces, you cover only 1½ miles (2½ kilometers) per hour on the flat.

Or perhaps you only need an extra hour for a 1200-foot (350-meter) climb; you could call that 50 minutes for 1000 feet.

If you kept a rough log of past trips, or have an unusually sharp memory, and still have the topo maps of the areas, you can work out your personal equation without putting on your boots.

James R. Wolf, whose climb and descent data for the entire length of the Appalachian Trail appear in volume II of *Hiking the Appalachian Trail*— a collection of tales by many through-hikers—gives this basic formula: 2.3 miles (3.7 kilometers) per hour plus one additional hour for each 700-foot (a bit more than 200-meter) rise. (I'm sure his pack was heavier most of the time than Mr. Wood's standard.) He also allows a correction—up to 15 percent plus or minus—for the condition of the trail.

Unfortunately, most of the time the condition of the trail cannot be read from the map. Any backpacker can recall some trail conditions that really slow you down. A packtrail out West, with a creek on one side, a cliff on the other, and overlapping prints of horses' hooves all over. Or a stretch of pancake-flat Florida Trail section through the Everglades with swamp on either side, all chewed up by line-abreast half-tracks. A scramble down a talus slope where every step releases a mini-avalanche of rocks. In winter, traversing breakable crust with nothing underneath it, with or without skis. . . . Mr. Wolf's 15 percent wouldn't begin to cover these situations.

Recently a study of hiking time and distance was made in Yosemite National Park. Jim Benedict, who was part of the project, reported some of the findings in *Backpacker 40*. Here are the formulas that approximate the measured results:

Up
Allow 30 minutes per mile.
For every 100-foot-per-mile-climb allow an extra 3½ minutes.

Down
Allow 30 minutes per mile.
For every 100-foot-per-mile drop allow 1 extra minute.

The next chapter shows how to get the climb or drop per mile.

Example. The trail climbs 600 feet in a mile. The formula gives 30 plus 6 × 3.5; that is, 51 minutes. Mr. Benedict's table gives 49 minutes.

Example. The trail drops 400 feet in a mile. The formula gives 30 plus 4 × 1; that is, 34 minutes. Mr. Benedict's table gives 33 minutes.

This system loses much of its simplicity in translation to metric units.

For metric readers, here is a formula given by Karl-schmidt in *Karte und Compass*. In flat country allow 10 to 15 minutes per kilometer. (That translates into 16 to 24 minutes per mile, or 2½ to 3¾ miles per hour.) In the mountains allow 15 additional minutes for every 100 meters climbed. (At 24 minutes for the flat mile, the example above works out to 52 minutes, almost too good a match with the formula for English units.)

For a 1000-meter altitude gain, the same booklet suggests allowing three hours, including short rests.

I have calculated five hikes in Austria with this metric formula. The sample included a cake walk and a real grunt. I know the conditions of the trails firsthand (or perhaps I should say firstfoot). They were all standard. The results agree reasonably well with the Yosemite table and with times on trail signs and on the back of Kompass maps.

Trail signs in the Alps, whether put up by alpine clubs or local authorities, invariably give walking time, not distance. One soon learns to multiply posted times by one's personal factor. On the hikes just mentioned, Trudy, my wife, and I took 25 percent longer than the signs said. You can use a similar simple adjustment to the result of any formula given here that appeals to you.

Whatever formula and correction you choose, they serve a double purpose. They let you figure the total walking time, and allow you to check between mapped landmarks on how you are progressing. At each landmark—peak, saddle, creek crossing, or whatever—you begin a new count to keep track of the distance traveled from that point.

On the overall walking time it pays to overestimate. When you tell your party, "It'll take about five hours," the figure becomes etched in their minds and the "about" is forgotten. Better make it six hours in your announcement, even if you think you'll make it in five if all goes well.

Even when you don't have to fear mutiny, I strongly suggest you overestimate when travel time is short. Say, when you didn't get to the trailhead until noon. It's specially important in winter, when days are short.

Table 3.2 will help you estimate the hours of daylight. It covers only fall and winter; the rest of the year the time from sunrise to sunset is at least 12 hours. You'll find the approximate length of day (in hours and tenths of hours) on the line of the nearest date in the column of the nearest latitude. For a margin of safety you can take the next greater latitude. (Table 12.3 provides the same information for southern latitudes.)

Example. November 15, latitude 45°N. Use November 17, latitude 45°N. You'll find 9.5 hours—that is, 9½

Table 3.2 Length of day in northern latitudes*

Date	20°N	35°N	45°N	52°N	56°N	60°N
Sept. 21	12.1	12.2	12.3	12.4	12.4	12.5
Oct. 1	12.0	11.9	11.8	11.7	11.6	11.5
11	11.8	11.5	11.2	11.0	10.8	10.6
23	11.6	11.1	10.7	10.3	10.0	9.6
Nov. 4	11.4	10.7	10.1	9.5	9.1	8.6
17	11.2	10.3	9.5	8.7	8.1	7.4
26	11.1	10.1	9.2	8.3	7.6	6.8
Dec. 11	10.9	9.8	8.8	7.8	7.1	6.0
Jan. 16	11.1	10.1	9.2	8.3	7.6	6.8
Feb. 2	11.3	10.5	9.8	9.1	8.6	8.0
14	11.5	10.9	10.4	9.9	9.5	9.1
25	11.7	11.3	10.9	10.6	10.4	10.1
Mar. 8	11.9	11.7	11.5	11.3	11.2	11.1
18	12.1	12.0	12.0	12.0	12.0	12.0

*Time between sunrise and sunset is given in hours and tenths of hours; one-tenth of an hour equals six minutes.

hours. In latitude 48°N you may want to use latitude 52° to get 8.7 or about 8¾ hours.

You'll get a slightly more accurate result by using a compromise between the earlier and the later date when the difference between dates is large.

Example. February 7, latitude 52°N. February 2 gives 9.1, and February 14 gives 9.9—a difference of 48 minutes. The compromise value of 9.5 hours is closer to the actual value.

In planning your day, don't forget to add the time before starting and the time it takes to set up camp in the evening when you fit your walking time into the available daylight hours.

4.
Height from the Map

You already know in a general way that the brown contour lines on topographic maps indicate elevations. Even without contour lines there are many spots on every topographic map where you can read the elevation directly.

Scattered all over our map are X-marks with the letters BM and a numeral. BM stands for bench mark, a surveyor's vertical control station. The center of the cross indicates the exact location, and the numeral gives the elevation in feet (or in meters on metric maps).

The starting point for measuring elevations used to be called mean sea level. That's the level of the ocean after eliminating the effect of waves and tides.

The waves are easy to eliminate. You set up a recording gauge in a protected corner of a quiet harbor and surround the float that drives your recorder with a box in which a few holes admit the water but not the waves.

The effect of the tides is eliminated by averaging hourly observations of sea level for about 19 years.

After that time the positions of sun and moon, and with them the tides, repeat themselves.

That may be interesting, but it's useless for measuring elevations in Colorado unless you can bring the sea level to these mountains by geodetic surveying.

That of course is what has been done. The new starting point, the *datum,* of elevations on modern United States topographic maps is called the National Geodetic Vertical Datum of 1929, a mean sea level adopted at that time.

You may have seen a round bronze disk set into the rock of a mountain peak. That was a bench mark. They are more common than mountain peaks. Every place in the contiguous United States is within one to three miles of a bench mark.

On our map they are all along the highway and the Grand Ditch.

They are not always as easy to see as on a mountain peak. They are placed, on purpose, where they are not likely to be disturbed. Surveyors and others with a need to know get the exact location from published data: so many feet west of the centerline of the road, for example, and so many feet north of somewhere else.

There are many more elevations printed on our map—on the peaks along the Continental Divide, for example.

You'll also see elevation figures on many section corners. It is indicated on the map by an upright red cross. The elevation refers to the position of that marker.

Horizontal control stations are marked on maps by an equilateral triangle with a dot in the center indicating the exact location. (Sorry, I can't find one on our map.) An elevation is often given next to it, with or without the letters BM. Occasionally you'll see the letters VABM, which stand for vertical angle bench mark. That refers to a less accurate method of surveying (but still more accurate than we shall ever need).

Some elevation figures are printed in brown rather than black. That indicates the elevations, taken from an earlier map, have not been rechecked.

Lake and river elevations are given in either blue or black. There is no special significance in the choice of color.

All these symbols and conventions are not restricted to topographic maps; you'll find them on planimetric maps. Even road maps give the height of some passes, peaks, and lakes.

You already know what makes topographic maps: contour lines. (Some authorities insist that the word *contours* refers to the shape of the land only; that on a map, and only on a map, the proper term is "contour lines." I don't think it's necessary to follow that rule when the meaning is obvious.) Before aerial photography and photogrammetry made maps with contour lines economical, shading and hachures—short lines drawn in the direction of the steepest slope, densest where the land was steepest—were used to convey the feel of the ups and downs of the land.

Some contour maps now are available with or without oblique shading, which adds a suggestion of a third dimension.

One such map is the one already mentioned of Rocky Mountain National Park. Figure 4.1 shows an area from this map that you can compare with our map. You can also compare it with Figure 4.2, which shows an orthophotoquad of the same area. The Grand Ditch and the Fall River Road will help you identify the other features shown.

The orthophotoquad, as you already know, is an aerial photograph straightened to national map accuracy standards, covering exactly the same area as the Fall River Pass quad from which our map is taken. Latitude and longitude are indicated just as on the contour map. Here the 1000-meter divisions of the Universal Transverse Mercator grid, discussed in the preceding chapter, are shown not just by ticks in the margins but by a network of lines over the entire map. A few place names have been added to aid in identification for people who are not as familiar with the area as you must be by now.

Interesting though these maps are for many purposes, for foot travel the regular quads are more useful.

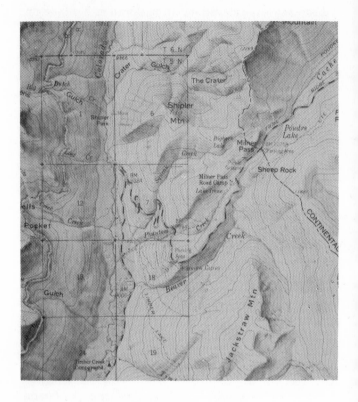

Figure 4.1 *Relief enhanced by shading of a topographic map. Compare this with the fold-out map at the back of this book.*

Contour Lines

If you can never remember that streams and lakes are blue on these maps, perhaps you are not as smart as your mother hoped you would be, but don't feel bad if you can't picture the landscape by looking at the squiggly brown lines. Sight-reading contour lines is not a skill we are born with or can acquire without effort. And it has nothing to do with smarts. Most people have to work at it until one day it becomes as natural as driving a car.

One way to help readers get the idea is to show a

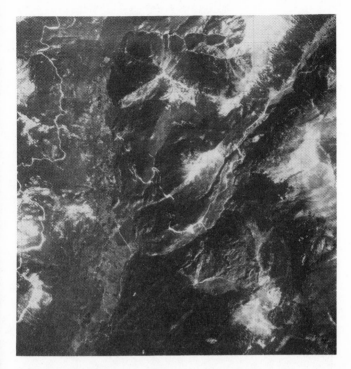

Figure 4.2 *Orthophotoquad of the area shown in Figure 4.1.*

landscape in perspective and the same landscape on a map with contour lines. Several authors have had that idea. In fact, half a dozen books on my shelves all use the same scene.

Let me try a different approach. I'll build a map of some very simple shapes before your eyes.

Humor me for a moment and pretend that the top sketch in Figure 4.3 is a volcanic island.

Now let's try to make a map of it. The first contour line to be drawn is the zero elevation line, the coastline at mean sea level. Obviously, if the island is as simple as I made it, that contour line will be a circle—a circle that connects all points of zero elevation. I'll call it zero feet, but here and in the next paragraphs you could read meters just as well.

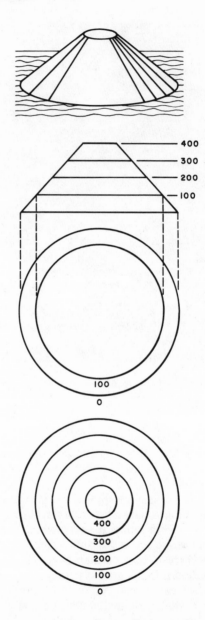

Figure 4.3 *Contours of a cone.*

Now let me melt some of the ice on Antarctica and raise the sea level 100 feet. The new contour line will be another, smaller circle that connects all the points 100 feet above the original sea level.

I'm still not satisfied and melt some more ice until the water has risen another 100 feet. The contour line will be a still smaller circle connecting all the points 200 feet above the original sea level.

Somehow I find more ice to melt. I raise the water another 100 feet, and then another 100 feet until it laps at the peak.

The contour line that connects all points 400 feet above the original sea level will be a very small circle.

If you didn't quite see how I got the contour lines, perhaps you'd rather imagine a papier-mâché volcano from your railroad set and take it with you in your bath for four days running. Each day you use less water in the tub than the day before. Let's have 12 inches of water the first day, 9 the next day, and so on. (The equal steps are not essential but make inter- pretation of the result easier.)

If you happen to be a chimney sweep you'll leave nice black rings in the bathtub and also on your moun- tain. The contour lines on a map can be thought of as an aerial view of such rings.

That last sentence is the key to the whole riddle of the brown squiggles. If you can see that, you are al- most there.

To go the rest of the way, let's tilt the cone of the first experiment, as shown in Figure 4.4. You can see that the right edge in the drawing is now steeper than the left.

Again I start by drawing the shoreline (at mean sea level), then raise the water 100 feet at a time, drawing contours just as before. Instead of circles they will form ellipses, like the figures your flashlight beam makes on the floor when you shine it at an angle rather than vertically.

If you have followed me this far, you are ready to deduce the first and most important rule about contour lines:

> Contours are closer together where the land
> is steep, farther apart where it is less steep.

Perhaps you found these mental experiments child-ish. There are no such mountains, at least not in Colo-rado—or are there?

Follow the Continental Divide from Milner Pass to-ward the bottom of our map. Does the first peak (un-named, at 11,881 feet) remind you of the tilted cone and its rings seen from above?

Less than a mile away (near latitude 40°25′N, longi-tude 105°47′30″W, marked by a black cross) is another unnamed peak, 11,961 feet high. Does it look familiar?

On our map, as on many 7½′ quads in the moun-tains, the contours are 40 feet (12 meters) apart. That corresponds to our raising the ocean 100 feet at a go,

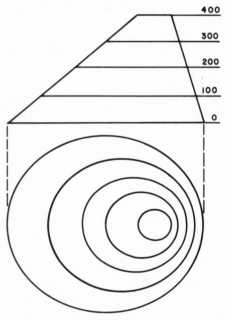

Figure 4.4 *Contours of a tilted cone.*

or bathing in three inches less water on consecutive days.

The contour interval is printed right on the map, usually directly below the graphic scales.

Even when the map is folded or the bottom margin has been cut off, you can get the contour interval from the lines themselves.

Find two numbered contours on your map. They'll be heavy lines, called index contours. In the top right corner you'll find one index contour labeled 10,800, and another, labeled near the lake, 11,000. So it's 200 feet between index contours. Next, count the spaces between the two lines. There are five, so the contour interval is 200÷5 or 40 feet.

Maps that use 25-foot contour intervals would have four spaces between index contours, 100 feet apart.

Not all maps of the 7½' series use the 40-foot contour interval. In southern Florida, one contour would be in one county and the next one two quads away in the next. Instead, a 10-foot interval might be used.

Sometimes you have to be careful to check whether elevations are increasing or decreasing. Often the blue color on the map is a quick aid. The Colorado River runs about from north to south on our map. Both banks, east and west of the flood plain, must be rising away from the river.

Poudre Lake and the Cache La Poudre River flowing out of it must also be low spots in their areas.

The area inside the last closed contour anywhere on a map leaves some doubt at times. Is the land still climbing, flat, or perhaps gently sloping?

The 11,881 and 11,961 peaks leave no doubt; each happens to be just one foot higher than the last contour. So the land, obviously, is not rising much.

If a lake were shown inside the last contour, I'd bet a dime the land was dropping. Without such a lake the drop would be shown on the map by one or more *depression contours,* contours sprouting short lines pointing downhill. Foreign maps may show a single arrow pointing down in this situation, much as an architect might show stairs leading to the basement.

It may help readers who still have trouble with the

basic concept of contours to see how contours were mapped—with much effort—before photogammetry became available.

A lot of points were surveyed. Their direction and distance from the stationary surveyor gave the location of the map points. The angle of his telescope together with the known elevation of the instrument gave the elevation of each point surveyed. That figure was written next to the point on the sheet.

Later, in the office, all the points with the exact elevation of a contour line, say 11,400 feet, were connected. Many points, of course, fell between contours. In drawing smooth curves the draftsman left higher points above and lower points below the line by as much as their difference from the elevation of the contour indicated. The process was similar to the way a meteorologist draws smooth isobars to fit the barometer readings from many stations.

More confused than ever?

I'll try one more experiment. Suppose you had a castle in the mountains. To protect it you might decide to build a moat around it and stock it with sharks.

How would you build it? Level, of course. If it ran up hill and down dale like the Great Wall of China, the water would not stay put. It'd run over the banks at low spots, leaving high spots dry.

If you had excess profits from your highway robberies, you might decide to build a second moat, say 100 feet below the first one. Again, it would have to be level.

With most topo maps that story would be a silly digression. But on our map the Grand Ditch is virtually such a moat, laid out near the 10,200-foot contour.

Do you see the connection between a water-filled moat and a contour line? Or the two moats in my fantasy and a contour interval of 100 feet?

Perhaps you have seen a model of some mountain landscape made of layers of plywood. Such a model illustrates the way contour lines work. And it is much easier to make than a true relief.

First you transfer contour lines—enlarged—from a topographic map onto pieces of plywood. You may want to use only every other contour line or only index contours to make your job easier. You then cut the plywood along the lines on a jigsaw. (All contours curve back on themselves, unless they run off the edge of the map.) Then you assemble the cutouts one on top of the other, and you have your model.

A bit crude perhaps, but quick. You could use the layered model as an armature for a true relief map—just smear modeling clay on the steps with a putty knife to change them to smooth slopes.

You can find illustrations of the rule about contour spacing—close where the land is steep, far apart where it is almost flat—in many places on our map.

The best example is the Colorado River valley. Near the river the lines are far apart, indicating fairly flat land. On the west bank, especially in section 12, and on the east bank, especially in section 6, the map is brown with closely spaced contour lines.

Now look at Shipler Mountain in section 6. Find the nameless creek that runs into the Colorado. Look at the contours in the vicinity of that creek. You'll notice the otherwise rather smooth curves taking a sharp turn in toward higher elevations and then turning out again.

That configuration is common at mountain creeks. Look, for example, at Lost Creek, which enters the Colorado just about opposite the unnamed creek. Or look at Squeak Creek in section 7.

Look at Shipler Mountain again. About a half mile north of the source of the nameless creek begins a set of other, rather gentler, bends in the contours pointing to lower elevations. They indicate a ridge, a mountain spur.

We can now offer a second rule about contour lines:

> In valleys, bends in contours point to higher elevations and are usually V-shaped.
> On ridges, bends in contours point to lower elevations and are usually U-shaped.

Figure 4.5 illustrates that rule. But things are not always so simple. The ridge between the unnamed creek and Squeak Creek is a good example of U-shaped bends in the lower reaches above the road. But at the

10,600 contour and above the bends become rather V-shaped; but they still point downhill, so they can't belong to a valley. Look again at Squeak Creek at the same contour line and notice how it bends uphill.

You'll never see a creek running along the top of a ridge. But don't expect every valley to have its own creek, a mapped blue line.

There is a third generalization we can make about contour lines:

> Contour lines are everywhere at
> right angles to the steepest slope.

A skier would say at right angles to the fall line. For the benefit of nonskiers, that's not where the skier falls, spills, craters, sitzmarks, washtubs, or whatever. Rather, it is the line a smart grand piano on skis would choose to end its misery: the shortest way down. That would be the same direction the artist would have drawn his hachures to indicate the trend of the slope.

It helps some people visualize the shapes of mountains to think of lines at right angles to the contour lines. See if that works for you. Start with the straight cone in Figure 4.2, then the tilted one in Figure 4.3,

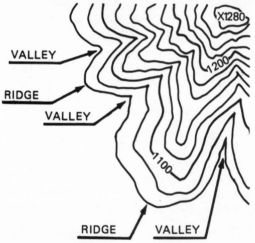

Figure 4.5 *Contours of ridges and valleys.*

then look at different areas of our map. Start with some simple feature, say the west bank of the Colorado, then try the two unnamed peaks, and graduate with some highly irregular shape, such as Shipler Mountain as a whole.

Later, in the chapter on navigation by altimeter, I'll show you how that simple third rule may help you orient yourself even when the visibility is rotten.

Reading the Slope

Can we tell from a topo map how steep a trail is? Certainly.

Suppose someone wanted to know how steep the Trail Ridge Road was between Fairview Curve and Milner Pass. You might talk your friend into accepting a figure starting just before the Phantom Creek crossing rather than from the curve. First you measure the distance with a pipe cleaner and get about 2.8 miles. You then calculate the difference in elevation from the two bench marks: 10,758 at the top, 9994 at the bottom—a difference of 764 feet. Divide the difference in elevations by the distance, and you get about 270 feet per mile on an average.

But using only bench marks on a topographic map is like using your hiking boots for doorstops. There are better uses for maps and boots. (It could also be said that I want to steer you away from checking the bench marks at the Grand Ditch. You'd find it really isn't a level castle moat, but slopes some 30 feet between the extreme bench marks on our map.)

Let's work some examples of measuring and calculating slope from contour lines.

Example 1. What is the slope of the Ute Trail, which we used to practice measuring distance in Chapter 3, between the Fairview Curve and Milner Pass? (A distance of about 1.9 miles.)

The trail starts about one and a half contour intervals—call it 60 feet—below the 10,200-foot index contour. Call it 10,140 feet. The last contour the trail touches, just before recrossing the road, is the one below the 10,800 index contour, the 10,760-foot level. (That checks nicely with the nearby bench mark elevation of the pass, 10,758 feet).

The trail rises 620 feet in about 1.9 miles.

We can express that better in several ways. For example, 1.9 miles at 5280 feet per statute mile equals 10,032 feet; that divided by 620 feet gives about 16. The trail rises, on the average, 1 foot in 16 feet, or 1 meter in 16 meters.

You can also divide the other way round, 620 ÷ 10,032, to get 0.06. A highway engineer would call it a 6 percent grade. The trail rises 6 feet in 100 feet, or 6 meters in 100 meters.

Yet another way is the one used in the last chapter to estimate walking time—rise in feet per mile. To get that you divide 620 feet by 1.9 miles and get 326 feet per mile for an average.

Example 2. What is the average grade and foot-per-mile rise on the Red Mountain Trail, from where you left your car near the buildings at the eastern border of section 12 to where the trail joins the road along the Grand Ditch?

If you really want to learn the business, you should work that problem yourself, then check your answer against the figures that follow.

For distance you should get about 3¼ miles, as we did in Chapter 3. For starting elevation you probably used 9040 feet (the stub end of the dirt road is right at that contour). The end of the trail here is above the 10,200 index contour but below the next one. Call it 10,220 feet. That makes the rise 1180 feet.

The distance is 17,160 feet (3¼ miles at 5280 feet per mile). Divide that by the rise and you get about a 1:14½ average grade. Divide the other way and you get about .07, or a 7 percent average grade. The simplest calculation of all is the rise in feet per mile. Divide the rise by 3.25 miles, and you'll get about 360 feet per mile.

Example 3. What's the total rise on a beeline scramble from your car to the Grand Ditch, shortcutting the Red Mountain trail? How steep is it?

The easiest way to answer the first question is to

count spaces between contour lines you would cross on that climb. You can use that technique regardless of the angle at which you would cross the contours.

You'll find a magnifying glass and a pointer, say a pine needle, helpful in counting. You'll also save a lot of eyestrain by counting, where possible, by spaces between index contours and then multiplying the result with the number of intervals between index contours, here five.

I count four spaces to the first index contour; then five spaces between index contours; and finally about half a contour interval to the road that parallels the Grand Ditch.

You could figure 4 spaces of 40 feet, plus 5 times 200, plus 20 feet gives 1180 feet. You could also figure 4 plus 5 times 5 plus ½ gives 29½ contour intervals of 40 feet, or 1180 feet. (That of course is the same result as in Example 2, where we subtracted the elevation at the bottom from that at the top.)

The counting and calculations are easier than the scramble. The straight-line distance, as you can check, is only 0.7 miles.

That makes the rise close to 1700 feet per mile, a steep 1:3 or 32 percent grade, overall.

But that average does not tell the whole story. After an easy start comes a 400-foot climb in a 600-foot distance, corresponding to a rise of 3500 feet per mile.

How did I measure that?

By putting a ruler across the brownest area—between 9400 and 9800 feet—and transferring the distance between these two contours to the graphic scale. I used the metric side of my ruler and got 8 millimeters; you could have used the other edge and got 5/16 inch.

If I had to do this kind of measurement often, I'd make my life easier by cutting out a template similar to those shown in Figure 4.6. Then, depending on the spacing of the contours, I'd put one of the three slots of that gauge across them *at the angle at which I will cross them*. I then count the lines in the slot and multiply with the factor next to the slot. The result is the rate of climb or descent in feet per mile.

Figure 4.6 shows two templates: one for the 1:24,000 scale, used on 7½' topo maps, and 40-foot contour intervals; the other for the 1:62,500 scale, used on 15' quads, and 80-foot contour intervals.

Measurements for cutting the slots are given in millimeters and tenths of a millimeter. I'm well aware that you can't cut to tenths of a millimeter, but it gives you a chance to shade your measurements. For example, 13.4 is about 13½ millimeters; 26.8, a shy 27 millimeters.

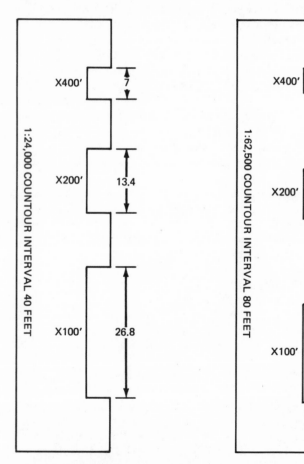

Figure 4.6 *Slope gauges.*

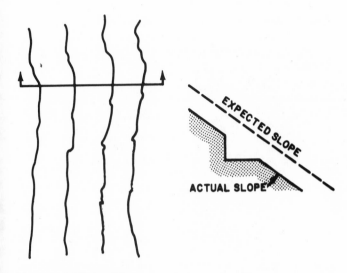

Figure 4.7 *Hidden cliff.*

In Figure 4.6 above, you would use the gauge on the left (1:24,000). The slot labeled "×400'" gives a shy nine contour intervals in the direction of travel—that is, straight across. Multiply that by 400 and you get a slope of 3600 feet per mile.

If you make gauges for both 7.5' and 15' quads, make sure you use the right one or you'll be about 30 percent off in your estimates.

And don't forget that the gauge must be at the angle you are walking. You can see what a difference that makes by measuring, however roughly without the gauge, a section of the straight-line scramble and comparing it with the same elevation difference along the Red Mountain Trail.

Warning: however carefully you measure on the map, calculate average gradients, and so on, you could be in for a nasty surprise. Theoretically at least, a cliff a little less than 40 feet high could hide between 40-foot contours, just as a waterfall could account for most of the drop on a white-water river (Figure 4.7).

5.

Direction from the Map

Y ou already know the two crucial facts about directions and maps:

1. The maps we use show points in the landscape in the proper direction. A road that takes off at right angles from another shows on the map in the same way.
2. The maps we use have North on top.

Fine points: there are charts of entire oceans and maps of the world on which, for special reasons, angles are not that simply related to the real world. On the small areas of our topographic maps, however, the first rule is universally true far beyond the level of accuracy that interests us.

If North is on top, East is on the right, South at the bottom, and West on the left. These four *cardinal points*—that is, principal points—are a good start for memorizing directions.

To describe a wind direction or some other direction—such as the trend of a river or trail—you go one step farther to the *intercardinal* points, halfway between the cardinals, abbreviated NE, SE, SW, and NW. Few people will care to go to the three-letter directions, such as NNE between NE and N, or ENE between NE and E.

For precise directions, degrees numbered from 0° for North and running clockwise to back to 360° at North are much simpler.

That's a lot easier to learn than the old system, which called what you now refer to as 14° North-by-East one-quarter East. It's also more precise. The best you could do with the old system of "boxing the compass" was to describe a direction to the nearest three degrees. (That, by no coincidence, was also as close as you could keep a sailing vessel on course.)

Unlike the old timer, who had to memorize that after N×E¼E came N×E½E followed by N×E¾E and NNE, all you have to know is that after 14 comes 15, followed by 16, and so on.

Directions in Degrees

I strongly urge you to learn a few key directions expressed in degrees. That'll keep you from making gross errors, such as marching off in exactly the opposite direction.

There are two methods to help you with that. The first is based on nothing more complicated than learning the figures that correspond to the four cardinal points: 0° (or 360°) for North, 90° for East, 180° for South, and 270° for West.

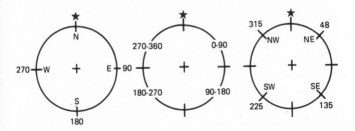

Figure 5.1 *Compass degrees.*

You can readily see from Figure 5.1 that any direction between North and East must be in the range of numbers from 0° to 90°, between East and South in the range of 90° to 180°, and so on.

Since most mistakes are errors of 180°, or more rarely of 90° or 270°, these four figures for the cardinals will catch most mistakes.

You can refine that system if you care to memorize the degrees that correspond to the intercardinals as well: NE, 45°; SE, 135°; SW, 225°; NW, 315°.

Many people find another system more to their liking. It's based on the familiar twelve-hour clock face. Multiply the hour by 30 and you have the corresponding degrees. For example, at three o'clock you get 90° (E), at nine o'clock you'll have 270° (W), and so on.

With that system you can check the approximate direction from Milner Pass to the following points:

Unnamed twin peak, 11,961 feet
Unnamed twin peak, 11,881 feet
Shipler Mountain
Peak west of Lake Irene, 11,209 feet

Just imagine the clock face centered on the pass. The first peak is a bit past three o'clock, therefore the direction is a little more than 90°. The measured directions are, in order, about 95°, 143°, 292°, and 240°.

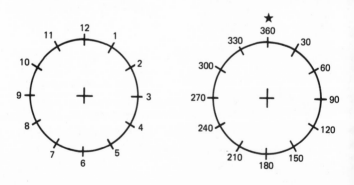

Figure 5.2 *Clock face and compass degrees.*

Measuring Directions on Maps

Sailors have it easy. Their charts (that's nautical for maps) have compass roses, marked in degrees, printed at convenient places all over the chart. To transfer lines from or to a compass rose, for measuring or plotting directions, marine navigators use parallel rules, two triangles, or drafting machines. But our maps have no compass roses.

Marine charts also have meridians and parallels of latitude printed on them. That allows you to use many kinds of protractors—long rectangular ones, square ones (large and small), and movable ones with or without arms.

Our maps have ticks in the margins and crosses in the map area itself where meridians and parallels of latitude cross. And that's it.

You could use a small movable-arm protractor by using the map margins to align it for North. But you won't see them much along the trails.

One protractor I could recommend consists of a square transparent plate with a degree scale with a string attached to its center. This gadget, made for small-plane navigators, is less than 5 inches (12 centimeters) square and weighs all of ½ ounce (15 grams). I can't tell you the price; I bought mine when coffee cost 5 cents.

It's simple to operate. Make sure N for North is on top of the plate. Align any edge of the protractor plate with any margin of the map and use the string as a straight edge. You read the true direction where the string crosses the 360° scale.

But you can get along fine without any protractor. Modern compasses—the type with a rectangular, transparent base and a compass needle in a housing that you can turn—serve as protractors.

Here is a standard problem: in what direction is point B from point A? Or less frighteningly put: in what direction should I move to get from where I am (on the map) to where I want to be? A navigator might call it the *course*.

There's another common problem: what mountain, lake, village, or whatever is it that I see over there?

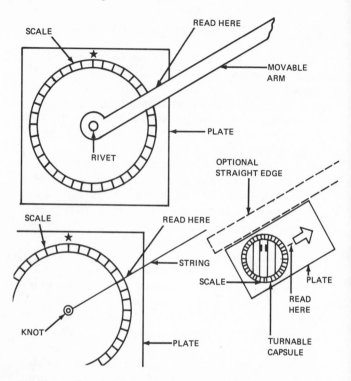

Figure 5.3 *Protractors. Top: moveable arm type. Bottom: string type. Right: a base plate compass acts as its own protractor.*

You can get an estimate of the direction of the object you want to identify with any compass. With some compasses you can measure the direction quite accurately. A navigator would call it a *bearing,* or, if he is given to fancier words, an *azimuth.*

You can see that this is very closely related to the course-finding problem. The question is: what mountain, lake, village, or whatever would I reach if I walked straight on that course?

Here's how modern compasses act as protractors, say, in finding a course.

Place either long edge of the compass on the map to connect the two points of the problem. Call them A and B, or start and destination. The arrow on the base plate, called the direction-of-travel arrow, quite logically must point to your destination. Or from A to B, not from B toward A.

Ignore the compass needle, but turn its enclosing capsule so the N mark points upward and the parallel lines are parallel with the left or right margin of the map. (Instead of the N mark your compass may have two parallel lines forming a gate for the North-pointing end of the magnetic needle, or some other device, such as two dots that glow in the dark to frame the luminous end of the needle.)

You can now read your course on the 360° scale at the bottom of the travel arrow.

You can see how the compass has acted like a protractor with a movable arm or a string. Perhaps you can't see how to align the lines of a compass capsule with the margins of the map accurately when the compass is somewhere in the middle of the map.

There is a method. It is shown in Figure 5.3 and uses the dime store ruler I suggested earlier as an aid to navigation:

1. Place the ruler on the map between A and B with one end of the ruler reaching the left or right margin of the map.
2. Place the compass alongside the ruler with one of its long edges touching the ruler and the direction-of-travel arrow pointing toward the destination, B.
3. Slide the compass along the ruler to the margin and turn the capsule, North mark up, until one of the parallel lines is parallel with the map margin.
4. You can now read the course on the degree scale at the base of the travel arrow.

Some people hate any sort of mathematics and may wonder if there is a way to do your compass work without any figuring.

Good news: yes, there is. In fact, there are several.

First off, there is the common use of compasses, especially by beginners. You only use it for such mundane purposes as deciding which fork in the road to take, or which of two trails. But you'd hardly call that navigation.

Then there is the problem dear to all writers of instruction booklets for compasses: walking toward a visible landmark. That sounds as if you did not really need a compass at all. But the idea is that on the way you'll lose sight of your goal. Then a compass lets you continue straight toward it, as if you could still see it.

In a narrow strip that now runs roughly from Lake Superior to Florida, and in a few other areas of the world, you could work the course problem by simply following the magnetic needle's direction. In a similar way, you could lay your compass on the map to decide what landmark you were looking at without any figure work. You'll read about these techniques in Chapter 7, "Using your Compass."

But most likely you will not always be in one of these strips that make compass work so easy. Elsewhere, as you probably remember, the compass needle points to West or East of true North. You must correct for that error.

The cheapest solution that takes little work is to apply the correction by adding it to or subtracting it from the course shown by the compass. You'd apply it to bearings by the opposite operation—subtracting or adding the correction. That can't be done without math.

But there are two ways out of that.

One costs money. You can buy a compass that, once set for the error (called *declination* ashore, *variation* at sea), eliminates the mathematics from courses and bearings.

The other solution takes work. After you find out what the local declination is, you line your map with a lot of parallel lines at that angle. Then you use these lines to set your compass capsule instead of aligning it with the map margins.

For now, simply remember this: (1) some compasses can act as protractors, and (2) almost nowhere does the compass needle point toward true North.

Position Lines

Perhaps now would be a good time to philosophize a little about land navigation.

You can, of course, learn all sorts of different routines without connecting one with the other. But many people learn and remember better when they can 'see the relation of one procedure with all others.

The unifying concept in navigation is the notion of lines of position. I have written a book for yachtsmen called *Practical Navigation* that uses this concept for everything from steering toward a lighthouse to electronic depthfinding and celestial navigation.

I prefer the shorter term *position lines*, and had expected some complaints about that. But not one reviewer or letter writer objected, so that's the term I'll use here too.

Simply put, a position line is a line (in nature or on the map) on or near which you are at the moment, without knowing how far along the line you are.

Suppose you get on a Fifth Avenue bus. As you bump along you are certain you are on that avenue. But, being a stranger in town, you don't know just where on Fifth Avenue you are at any given time. A typical position line situation.

Then you see a street sign: 42nd Street. Your doubts are dissolved. You can think of that street as another position line.

You are on both these position lines at once, so you must also be at the point on the map where the two cross. In nautical language, which in this case is worth adopting for our use, you have a *fix.*

That is land navigation, but hardly what you had in mind when you opened this book. All right, here's an example closer to our subject. You are hiking a well-established, mapped trail. You have been going for some time. You are sure you're on the right trail, but how far have you come?

Now you cross a stream, clearly shown on the map. There is no other stream crossing within many miles.

Again, you are on two position lines at the same time, one the trail and the other the stream. Your position is pinpointed: you have a fix.

A power line, a cross trail, a fork in the trail, a saddle, entering or leaving a National Forest or a Wilderness Area (according to a trail sign)—these and many other landmarks would do as well to fix your position.

Another example: you walk a compass course in open terrain. You are sure of your direction, but the distance covered gets more doubtful with every hour you walk. Say the formula you use estimates distance accurately within ½ mile per hour; after three hours, the possible error is 1½ miles. You could be that distance ahead of or behind your calculated distance. An uncertainty of 3 miles (5 kilometers).

A marine navigator would call a similar position derived from course, speed, and time his *dead reckoning* position, or *DR* (a term supposedly derived from "deduced reckoning"). I think that's another term we might adopt.

Now you notice two peaks on your right, one near, one more distant, coming almost into one line. You keep going until they exactly line up. Draw a straight line through the two peaks on the map and across your track. Again, being on two position lines at once, you are at their crossing point on the map.

Or near it, at least. However carefully you tried, you probably did not follow the compass course exactly. And what seems to be the peak may be a point near it.

There are not enough such "transits" of two objects to navigate by. But with some compasses you can take bearings accurately enough to get good position lines.

On a mapped trail, one such bearing gives you a fix. (You may take a second bearing on another object as a check.) Off-trail, or when you don't know which trail you're on, the intersection of two bearings can pinpoint your position.

Obviously the two bearings must be at different angles from you. Two objects in the same direction (angle 0°) or exactly opposite each other (angle 180°) are no better than a single bearing. The ideal lies halfway between these extremes. Try for bearings that differ by 90°. Usually you won't find two objects lined up just so, and you must settle for any angle between 45° and 135°—that is, 90° plus or minus 45°.

Contour lines in combination with a little precision instrument that tells your present elevation, an *altimeter*, open up more position lines.

The trail you're on could be one position line, the

contour line corresponding to your elevation the other.
There usually is only one spot where they cross, and
there is always only one where they cross for the first
time. That's your fix.

You don't even need a trail. Say you are hiking
cross-country. Your elevation gives one position line;
the other can come from a creek, a mapped fence, or
the bearing of a peak you recognize.

You'll read much more about these techniques in
Chapter 10, "Altimeter Navigation." You'll even read
about a method that can often get your position on the
map from an accurate altimeter reading and nothing
else—no trail, creek, or fence—without any visible
landmarks.

Converging Map Margins

Some sharp-eyed readers will have noticed that the
margins of the map of Colorado, in Figure 3.1, converge. So of course do all the meridians on a globe.
You may have wondered whether the margins on 7½'
and 15' topographic maps converge. Yes, they do—a
little.

If you align the South edge of the 7½' quad from
which our map was taken with that map's North edge,
you'll find it 1/32 inch (3/4 millimeter) longer. On a 15'
quad in the same latitude, the difference would be
about 60 percent larger. On the Rocky Mountain National Park map, on the same scale as the 15' quads but
taking in almost twice as much latitude and longitude,
the difference between North and South margins is
about 5/32 inch (4 millimeters).

Strictly speaking, we should align our compass with
the left margin when the angle measured is near the
left margin, and with the right margin when it's near
the right. But the error caused by the convergence of
the meridians in these small areas is well below the accuracy you expect or need. (The angle between one of
the side margins and a vertical line through the center
of the Rocky Mountain National Park is on the order
of one-eighth of a degree.)

The compasses used for land navigation typically are

calibrated at two-degree intervals. But that brings us to the next chapter, where you'll meet a representative collection of these protractor compasses.

6.
Choosing a Compass

This chapter is about compasses, especially the kind suitable for most outdoor activities.

Any compass, right down to the gumball machine model, lets you turn the map so that it approximately matches what you see in the field. It also lets you decide which branch of a trail leads East, which South. Other compasses let you do a lot more.

For our purposes the choice is between the many compasses that act as their own protractors, to which you were introduced in the last chapter. They are often referred to as "orienteering" compasses.

I use the term reluctantly. For one thing, many readers will think that's a silly adjective to hang on a compass. It's like saying "a time watch." Aren't all compasses used to orient yourself? For another, the word *orienteering* has been registered as a trademark by the Silva Company, now a division of Johnson Wax Associates.

In a recent edition of a book by the founder of Silva, you'll find this notice: "ORIENTEERING is a coined word, registered in the U.S.A. and Canada for services rendered and products distributed by Orienteering Services/U.S.A., Binghamton, N.Y., and by Orienteering Services/Canada, Willowdale, Ontario Canada."

One may wonder about it being a "coined word." Would the first hospital that sent a bill for a kidney transplantation, which sounds more expensive than a mere transplant, apply for a trademark? The term was used in Norway in 1900, some 30 years before these compasses came into being.

Finally, there is a competitive sport called orienteering—a combination of jogging and map and compass work. (Orienteering Services provides training materials and equipment for this sport.) People who participate in the sport use these compasses, but so do hikers, skiers, fishermen, and many others.

And with good reason: these compasses are more versatile, faster, and handier—once you have learned to use them—than any other kind.

You could call them protractor compasses. Or perhaps base plate compasses, as some importers of Suunto and other compasses do.

The only good argument I've heard for other types of compass—pocket, pin-on, or wrist—is for a cross-country skier who'd rather glance at a pin-on than take off gloves, unzip pockets. . . . As a backup in case you lose your base plate model, they don't rate; a serviceable compass of these types costs about the same as an inexpensive base plate compass.

All members of the party—except small children—should have their own compasses. If you, Mr. Tourguide, lose yours, you can always commandeer one.

All these compasses fit in a breast pocket (sizes run about 2½ by 4 inches, or 6 by 10 centimeters) and will fall out when you lean over. However, all but the least expensive models come supplied with lanyards to keep your compass from losing you. Even the inexpensive compasses provide for attaching a lanyard; you have to supply the string and knot it.

I will describe the variety of base plate compasses available to make it easier for you to follow the detailed instructions in the next few chapters. But I suggest you delay your final decision until you have looked at those chapters.

Basic Types of Base Plate Compasses

The choice of base plate compasses is bewildering. A single manufacturer, Silva of Sweden, shows 11 models in a brochure, most of which look much alike. Another manufacturer, Suunto of Finland, shows almost as many, and they not only look alike but also match Silva's in many details.

You can make your selection much easier—for the moment, at least—by disregarding minor conveniences: rubber feet to keep the compass from sliding off the map; built-in magnifiers (some supposedly capable of lighting fires in an emergency, if the sun is shining); clinometers, which measure the steepness of a slope; and a gadget you click each time you have walked 100 paces.

At this stage I would also disregard the minor differences in size and weight. I yield to nobody in my aversion for carrying a load, but one has to draw the line somewhere. (If you cut the string off tea bags, you have to carry extra burn dressings.)

Compasses come with a bewildering number of scales on as many as three edges. Inches (divided into eighths or tenths) and centimeters (divided into millimeters) are common; also miles and kilometers in a variety of map scales. Some have interchangeable scales.

Don't select a compass for its scales any more than you'd buy an automobile for its neat rear-view mirror. Your ruler, pipe cleaner, or fingers can substitute. You can also cut the graphic scale of your choice from a map and glue it on your compass.

Even the divisions of the degree scale, which make these compasses into protractors, don't matter terribly much. Some compasses are graduated in five-degree intervals, most of them in two-degree steps.

If you can bring yourself to disregard these minor points, I can narrow down the choice to a few models. They are all top quality. That's not just my personal opinion, but is backed up by an article in *Backpacker 13*.

(Only a few models have been added or slightly improved since then.) The tests used for the article included dropping each compass onto a blanket atop a cement block from a height of 10 feet (about 3 meters) three times.

All the compasses mentioned below were rated ***** excellent, or at least **** superior.

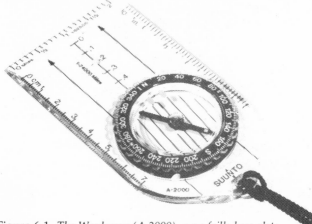

Figure 6.1 *The Woodsman (A-2000), a no-frills base plate compass.*

Figure 6.2 *Silva® Type 7, another basic protractor compass.*

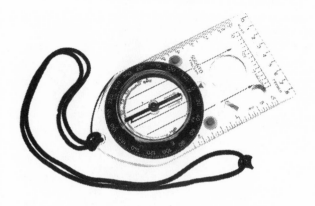

Figure 6.3 *The Leader (M-3D), with declination adjustment worked with key seen on the lanyard.*

Figure 6.4 *Silva® Type 20, a mirror-sight compass.*

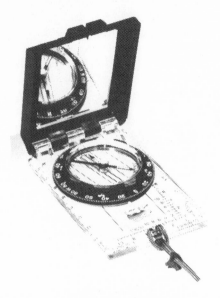

Figure 6.5 *The Professional (MC-1D), a mirror-sight compass with declination adjustment and clinometer.*

Figure 6.6 *Silva® Type 15 is like the Type 20, but has a declination adjustment and built-in clinometer.*

All the models on my list are liquid damped for bringing the needle to rest quickly. The needles in hand-held air-filled models never really stop their jitters, and you may have water seepage troubles with these compasses. They also need a needle lifter mechanism to save wear on the needle bearing.

All the models on my list have jeweled bearings.

The liquid in these compasses freezes at about $-40°F$ ($-40°C$). An occasional *small* air bubble in the liquid does not affect the performance of the compass. If you get a large bubble, return the compass. (All are guaranteed for one year.) If the liquid doesn't get out, water can't get in either.

The bottom of the capsule that houses the compass needle is transparent. That lets you align the capsule with map margins or whatever, as discussed a little in the last chapter and in detail in the next few chapters.

The North end of the needle is clearly marked, though not necessarily with the letter N, which was fashionable at one time. More often you match the shape and color of the end of the needle with a corre-

Table 6.1 Base plate compasses

A Point compass for taking bearings

Weight 1–2 ounces (30–60 grams)	*Price (1989)*	*Illustration*
You correct for declination		
Woodsman (Suunto A-2000)	$ 9	Figure 6.1
Silva® Type 7	$10	Figure 6.2
Set and forget about declination		
Leader (Suunto M-3D)	$16	Figure 6.3

B Mirror sight for taking bearings

Weight 2–4 ounces (60–120 grams)	*Price (1989)*	*Illustration*
You correct for declination		
Silva® Type 20	$16	Figure 6.4
Set and forget about declination		
Professional (Suunto MC-1D)	$32	Figure 6.5
Silva® Type 15	$44	Figure 6.6

sponding design in the capsule. That makes the identification of the correct end of the needle just about idiotproof.

All but the least expensive models have luminous points that help in night work. Unless you have a light of your own you should probably not be walking around in the dark anyway. A luminous compass will not prevent you from turning an ankle.

The prices (1989) are for guidance only. Even though they are likely to change, they give an indication of how much each step up may add.

Now to the decisions. There are two you need to make.

First, will you be satisfied with taking bearings by merely pointing the base plate of the compass at the target?

According to the expert who evaluated the compasses for *Backpacker*, that should get you within four degrees, for a total error of probably not more than eight degrees.

For identifying a feature in the landscape, that's probably good enough. (An error of four degrees to either side is about the distance on the horizon covered by four of your fingers, arm outstretched.)

Over a distance of one mile, a four-degree error amounts to being 380 feet off to one side or the other. Over three miles, that makes an error on the order of 1200 feet. (In metric units: over a distance of one kilometer, a four-degree error amounts to about 70 meters off to one side or the other. Over five kilometers, that makes an error on the order of 350 meters.)

For fixing your position accurately, such bearings are poor—and the farther the target of your bearing, the worse it gets. I'll go into that in more detail later.

If your answer is "Yes, it's good enough," pick a compass from section A in Table 6.1. If not, go to section B.

The other question you need to ask is: are you willing to correct for declination for every course and every bearing by calculation or by drawing lines on your maps?

If yes, choose a compass from the top of either A or B.

If, on the other hand, you want to set your compass for the declination in the region and then forget all about it, choose from the lower part of A or B.

My bias is for the bottom of B because I want to have the option of using bearings for fixing my position, and because I want to read bearings and courses directly from my compass. It's not the work of figuring that makes me pick from the bottom of the table. I'm more concerned that sometime, tired and wet perhaps, I'll add when I should be subtracting. (It's easy to get confused—in one area you add to courses, subtract from bearings; in another you subtract from courses, add to bearings.)

If you do it wrong it's serious. Say the declination is 15°. If you do the figuring wrong you'll be 30° off. That's 3000 feet over a distance of one mile (580 meters per kilometer).

The advantage of the set-and-forget system is that you don't have to work with numbers at all. You get courses off the map and walk them by compass, unconcerned about how many degrees from North that is. Or you take a bearing and plot it on the map without ever having to read the degree scale.

Fine Points to Consider

Dip

You should buy your compass where it is to be used. I don't mean you should not use a compass bought in Idaho in Montana or the other way round. But the compass that gave you good service in the United States will hang up in Australia.

Let me explain. The earth's magnetic field not only dictates the direction of the compass needle, it also makes it dip (toward the North in the United States). This effect is known as *dip,* or, if you must have a longer term, *magnetic inclination.*

Imagine a compass needle arranged not as in a compass, but free to take any position in a vertical plane. Only along a line known as the magnetic equator will the needle point horizontally. This line gently curves around the geographic equator, staying roughly within 10°N and 15°S.

As you get farther from that line, the dip generally increases. In Australia it is between 40° and 70° toward the South. In the United States, southern Canada, and Europe it is 55° to 75° toward the North.

Compass makers overcome the tendency of the needle to point toward the bottom of the capsule by counterbalancing the needle, sometimes using nothing more complicated than a drop of paint.

If you plan to climb in Chile, buy your compass there; or order one for use in that area before you leave home.

Types of Scales

The compasses we are talking about come with a 360° scale as a rule, in the United States at least. But there are other scales. Some surveyors prefer a scale that runs four times from 0° to 90°. Others insist on 400 subdivisions, called *grads*, in place of the 360°. A right angle in that system is, of course, 100 grads. Making a 180° turn becomes making a 200.

Worse yet are *mils*. They are optional alongside degrees on some compasses, the only markings on others.

If you drew a circle with a 1000-foot (or 1000-meter) radius it would have a circumference of about 6283 feet (or 6283 meters). That provides a basis for dividing the whole circle. The divisions are much finer than mere degrees, which appeals to the military. But dividing the circle into that odd number was just too much. So they divided it in 6400 divisions instead and called them mils. (To confuse the enemy, some nations have adopted 6000 divisions.)

The only place you'll encounter mils is in the declination diagram on topographic maps, where they are given alongside the same information in degrees. One degree equals about 18 mils.

The reason for mentioning all these strange scales is to prepare you for the questions of a salesperson and to avoid disappointment when you open the parcel containing your mail-order compass the day before your departure for Chile. You should ask for clockwise 360° scales.

Some top-of-the-line compasses come in their own cases. Personally I would pass up the optional cases for less costly instruments. The case sometimes weighs more than the compass and costs as much as one of the simple models that could act as a spare.

To protect the compass—or in the mirror models the bottom of the compass—from scratches, I use sandwich bags, which I carry for all sorts of other purposes, including sandwiches.

Compasses Designed for High Accuracy

When you shop for a compass you may see much fancier models than the simple models shown in Table 6.1 Before deciding on one of them, keep in mind that unless they have at least one straight edge corresponding to the long edges on a base plate compass they can't be used in the simple manner of the protractor compasses.

You may be tempted to get a compass that lets you take more accurate bearings than the mirror-sighting models permit. Lensatic (using lenses), prismatic (using prisms), and optical sighting compasses are used by the military and by timber cruisers and other professionals.

Unless such compasses are robust—which unfortunately often means heavy and expensive—their accuracy will prove an illusion.

I can't recommend a sighting compass, however well made, that does not let you take sights of peaks from the valley, or the valley from a peak. If you have to bring the peak down to your level mentally, you lose all of the accuracy for which you have paid.

There is one compass that lets you take sight of objects above or below you that's very popular in Europe but seldom seen in North America (perhaps because of its price, which is more than $100). The Bézard.

Named after its inventor Colonel von Bézard (emphasis on the last syllable), it is a sturdy aluminum model that weighs about 3½ ounces (105 grams). It has one rather short straight edge. A longer ruler attachment is available, but your dime store ruler will work fine with it too. Sighting is through a long slot in the cover.

The model you may want is #703, called Fluid Bézard. That, of course, means it is fluid damped; the capsule in that model is transparent to let you see the map underneath.

With this compass, invented in time to serve the armies in the First World War, you align the band inscribed "Fluid Bézard" with a horizontal margin of the map, rather than the usual vertical margin. You can also align it with any place name on the map. That's not too useful on our map, which has very few words printed horizontally. But on a map of Switzerland, for example, with place names all over the sheet, it is a quick method.

You are not likely to forget that the name of the

Figure 6.7 *The Bézard, a sturdy compass; note slits for sighting.*

compass must be right side up, not standing on its head.

The compass can be adjusted for local declination, and is adjusted at the factory for the declination of the place of sale. The adjustment requires a watchmaker's screwdriver. Three tiny screws in the compass capsule have to be loosened, and tightened again after adjustment. It's definitely an indoor job.

Besides the usual (luminous) arrangement for aligning the compass needle with a mark in the capsule, this compass has auxiliary marks 45° and 90° on either side of the main mark. To avoid obstacles, or to make a steep slope easier to climb with skis, snowshoes, or on foot, you change course first to one side, then to the other. These marks eliminate the mathematics from these maneuvers.

You may find these marks so handy that you'd like to add them to your own compass. On many of the base plate compasses that's quite easy to do.

Buying a Base Plate Compass

When you have decided on the model of compass you want, need, or can afford at the moment, by all means spend some time on the purchase. Unless you lose it, which is not likely if you use its lanyard, the compass will be with you for a long time.

However, if you don't live near a well-stocked mountain shop, don't hesitate to order a compass by mail. Any reputable mail order dealer will exchange a compass that fails any of the tests described below. Most of them will also understand if you don't like the feel of a specific model.

Just as the heft of a hammer or the feel of a screwdriver makes the difference between tools you feel comfortable with and tools that merely drive nails or turn screws, so one compass will suit you better than another of perhaps equal quality and price.

Look especially at the 360° scales. Some are easier to read than others. This has little to do with price. To my eyes the inexpensive Polaris has one of the most legible scales of all.

Then look at the North end of the needle and the design you are to match it with.

If you don't normally wear glasses outdoors, you shouldn't wear them for either of these tests.

When you have made your decision, the salesperson is likely to hand you a brand new compass. Test it.

It should have no bubbles in the liquid of the capsule. It should show North where other compasses in the store do. That sounds silly, but compasses sometimes switch polarity when they are stored close together; what should be the North-pointing end of the needle points South.

Next check how the capsule turns. If it hurts your fingers, get another specimen; perhaps a different model if the stiffness and sharp edges are family traits.

Next see if the capsule has excessive side play. Turn the compass until the needle is in the slot or whatever design that compass uses. Then try to move the capsule East and West. If the reading at the index mark changes more than one degree, try another compass.

If the compass has index marks both near and away from you, make sure they are in line. When one reads 180° the other should read 360° or 0°, not 358° or 2°.

Mirror-Sighting Compasses Only

Hold the compass horizontally in front of you and see if you can sight on an object near the ceiling (compass somewhat above eye level) and then on the floor a few feet away (compass somewhat below eye level) while watching the needle in the mirror. Unless you always operate in dead flat country, I cannot recommend any model that fails this test.

The bottom of the V-sight, the line on the mirror, the index mark (or marks), and the center of the needle pivot must all be in line. Just to make sure this specimen hasn't missed final inspection, try this one-eyed test. Hold the compass at about eye level before you. Tilt the mirror until you can see the entire capsule. Now turn the compass slightly sideways until the black line of the mirror seems to go through the center of the needle pivot and the near index mark.

Very likely you won't be able to see the far index

mark at the same time. But if the compass passed the 180°/360° test above, all is well so far.

Many mirror-sight compasses have molded into the cover a line running from the base of the V in the sight toward the line on the mirror. You can tell at a glance whether the lines meet at the upper edge of the mirror; if not, reject the specimen.

Declination-Adjusted Compasses Only

Have the salesperson show you how the declination adjustment works. Or ask to be left alone with the instruction book, which should be fairly clear on that subject.

Silva compasses are adjusted with a small screwdriver blade threaded on the lanyard. Suunto compasses have a small stud threaded on their lanyards that is inserted in a hole in the bottom for adjustment. The Touring compass is adjusted with your bare fingers by turning a bar at the base of the capsule.

I would make sure that the adjustment worked and that I knew how to work it. But I would not pick one make or model over another by how hard the adjustment is to set.

You won't have to adjust it very often. In the area of our map, for example, you'd readjust it after you had traveled 100 miles (160 kilometers) East or West, and after a much greater distance if you traveled North or South.

Automobile Compasses

Sometimes the hardest navigation is to the trailhead by back roads, where a forest map and a compass would help. You may not feel like getting out of your car and walking 30 feet (10 meters) away from it so your hiking compass can do some undisturbed navigation.

There are compasses specially made for automobiles. They are not terribly accurate—every steel part in an automobile attracts the magnetic element in the compass, and every direct current throws it off—but they are useful when properly placed and adjusted.

An automobile compass won't work right if you just

take it out of its box and mount it just any place. Read the instructions on where to place the compass and how to adjust it—that is, how to compensate for the car's magnetic fields, both mechanical and electrical. It usually works something like this:

1. Put the car on a heading of magnetic East. With a non-magnetic screwdriver (a dime, or a blade whittled from a piece of hardwood) make the compass read East by turning the screw usually marked E-W. If nothing happens you are turning the wrong adjusting screw. If the compass reading moves away from East instead of toward it, you're turning the right screw the wrong way.

2. Put the car on a heading of magnetic North. By turning the other screw, usually marked N-S, make the compass read North. If nothing happens you are turning the wrong screw and just have canceled the first adjustment. Start over. If the compass reading moves away from North instead of toward it, you are turning the correct screw the wrong way.

3. Put the car on a magnetic heading of West. With the first screw you used remove one half of the remaining error. If, for example, the compass indicates 10° from West, turn the East-West screw until the error is only 5°.

4. Put the car on a magnetic heading of South. Using the second screw, marked N-S, again remove half of the remaining error. And that's about the best you can do.

Make sure there are no overhead wires nearby that may influence your compass when you are adjusting it. Find the cardinal headings with your hiking compass with the car a good distance off so it won't throw off your hiking compass.

Don't expect a perfect adjustment. Check what various circuits in the car do to your adjustment. If you find, for example, that turning on the electric windshield wipers upsets your carefully performed adjustment, trust your compass only when the wipers are off.

Don't expect too much accuracy from any car compass and don't forget that if you move it, even only a hand's width, you have to readjust it all over.

When in doubt, walk away from your vehicle and use your protractor compass where it is not disturbed by automotive parts and electrical circuits (including those in transistor radios, exposure meters, and so on).

I would not necessarily buy the best automobile compass, judging by price. Even the best will not be very accurate once you install it in your vehicle. But it'll keep you from starting out in the wrong direction or taking the wrong fork—and so will a well-adjusted, less expensive compass.

7.
Using
Your Compass

In this chapter, in order to simplify things a bit, I'll assume we are in an area of virtually no declination, or are using a set-and-forget model already set for the local declination. How to find and live with declination is the subject of the following chapters.

All makes and models of base plate compasses are handled in the same manner. It's somewhat like driving a car. If you know how to drive a Chevrolet, you can also drive a Ford.

The only difference in compasses is in how you take a bearing: by looking at a mirror on some models, by just pointing the compass in others. That's comparable to the difference between a stick shift and an automatic transmission.

Leaving out such goodies as lanyards, magnifiers, fire starters, pace reminders, slope-measuring gadgets, and map scales, base plate compasses are fairly simple devices. Like other hand compasses, they have a magnetized needle that turns on a jeweled bearing on a pivot. The entire assembly is enclosed in a capsule that you can turn with respect to the base plate. Both the plate and the capsule are transparent to let you see the map underneath them.

A degree dial (azimuth ring) read against a stationary mark indicates how far you have turned the capsule. The mark is often at the base of an arrow that indicates the direction of travel or of sighting.

On folding mirror models the mirror is hinged where the arrow ought to start. A line (often luminous) acts as an index mark, and the mirror itself indicates the direction of travel. On some compasses you'll find a second index mark, perhaps also luminous, exactly opposite the main one.

A design corresponding to the end of the compass needle that points toward North is drawn on the top or bottom of the capsule. The details of the design vary. It may be an arrow (sometimes called orienting arrow), a gate formed by two bars, or any other pattern. It is often color coded to correspond with the red end of the needle. If the needle is luminous, as it is on all but the lowest-cost models, the arrow, gate, or whatever will also glow in the dark.

Now we need a term that describes the activity of putting the North end of the compass needle over the arrow, slot, or gate. I shall use the phrase *box the needle.* To me it has a nice nautical ring, reminiscent of "boxing the compass," used to describe the recital of compass directions in their proper order.

You'll box the needle a lot in this chapter and in using your compass. You can see that you can get the North end of the needle into its box in two ways. Either you turn the whole compass, or you turn only the capsule.

Sometimes you use one method and sometimes the other. It sounds confusing, but there is a very logical way to remember which method to use:

> If you have just set the capsule—in order to get a course off the map, for example—you turn the entire compass.

> If you have just turned the whole compass—in order to get the bearing of a peak, for example—you turn the capsule.

Parallel to the boxing mark on the top or bottom of the capsule, you'll find a set of lines. They are variously called *orienting lines, meridians*, or *North-South lines*.

You'll recall that meridians in geography are the lines that run from pole to pole on a map or a globe. You'll often be aligning the lines in the capsule with the meridians on your map.

On topo maps you'll usually have only two meridians: the left and the right margin of the quad. Often it's good enough to align the lines in the capsule with the margins of the map by the eyeball method. I'll show you another method for use when greater accuracy is needed.

Since North on maps is at the top, the mark that indicates North in the capsule must be at the top when you align the capsule meridians with the map meridians. (Later I'll refer to this activity simply as *aligning the meridians.*)

Preliminary Practice

After looking at your compass and checking to see

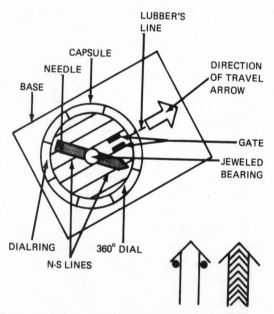

Figure 7.1 *Parts of a protractor compass.*

whether I missed any vital parts in my description, put it on a table and turn it. You'll discover that as you turn the base plate in any direction the needle stays still. An optical illusion may mask that fact: the turning meridian lines may seem to make the needle move. Put your finger where the needle points and you'll see that it keeps pointing at your finger.

On my desk you'd make another discovery. The direction of the needle changes depending where you put the compass down; and when you pull out the center drawer the needle turns almost 90°. The explanation: a pair of scissors in the drawer attracts the needle.

A knife, a paper clip, or anything made of steel, not to mention electric circuits such as those in pocket transistor radios, will have a similar effect. Moral: keep such items away from your compass. Belt buckles, even when they look like brass, are suspect. Check whether yours deflects the compass needle. The error caused by such influences on the compass needle is called *deviation*.

Next, if you have not yet tried it, practice boxing the needle by turning the capsule and by turning the base plate.

If you have a topo quad, put the compass down anywhere on it and align the meridians by eye only. If there are red survey lines on the map, you can use them as a guide.

If you don't have a map handy, use a newspaper. Pretend the left margin of the first column and the right margin of the last one are map margins.

First, place the compass in three different positions at random, the direction of travel arrow pointing every which way, and align the meridians. If, even once, you did not have the boxing mark at the top, make yourself stand in the corner for five minutes.

For the next practice you'll need a ruler or similar straightedge. Again, place the compass randomly and align the meridians by eye alone. But now go one step further. Slide the compass along one edge of the ruler toward the right or left map or column margin.

Are the lines in the capsule exactly aligned? If they are you have a better feel for the vertical than most people, or else you have just been lucky.

To eliminate the luck hypothesis, try this test a few more times with the base plate pointing nearly up or down and nearly left or right.

After a few tries, aligning the meridians becomes an almost automatic routine. And you won't forget to have the box on top.

You may object, "That works fine on my desk, but how do I do that while hiking?"

Like most hikers, you probably carry your map folded rather than rolled. If you carry it that way you can work the same system if you plan your folds.

Fold the map in half vertically, printed side out. Then fold it in thirds horizontally. On 7½' and 15' series quads, the thirds are marked clearly along both

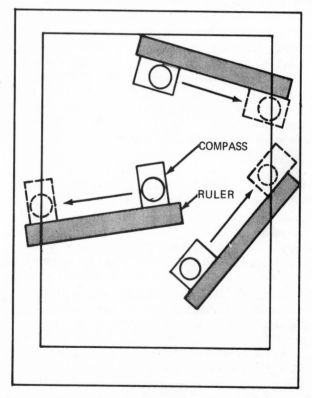

Figure 7.2 *Using compass and ruler on a map.*

vertical edges by ticks labeled with latitude, such as 25', 27'30", or 5', 10'.

Look for these markings. We'll use them in Chapter 9 to allow for declination at no expense and with relatively little work.

Serious Compass Work

We are now ready to practice map-and-compass work.

Normally we work with map and compass together. But the first technique of compass work described below needs no map.

Walking a Field Bearing

This involves using your compass to get the direction of your destination, then following the compass to get there.

Perhaps that does not make sense to you. Why would you need a compass to reach something in plain sight?

An example: you are standing on Milner Pass and want to climb one of the twin peaks, the one 11,881 feet high on our map. For some reason you want to do so by the most direct route. You may regret that choice of route; it climbs 1123 feet in 7/10 mile (340 meters in 1 1/10 kilometers). Not having a map, you don't know that. But you can plainly see that after just a few minutes you'll be in the woods and probably lose sight of the peak. (We know it because of the green tint on the map.) To find your way to that peak, or any other destination you may lose sight of during the journey, proceed as follows:

Step 1. Aim the direction-of-travel arrow of your compass at your target. Face your destination squarely and hold the compass horizontally, in your left hand if you are right-handed (you'll need your right in the next step), and chest-high.

When the target is higher than you are, it helps to look at the peak, then down toward the compass, and back up at the peak. If the target is lower than you are, say a lake seen from a peak, you may be able to look at it through the base plate, which makes accurate aiming easy.

With a mirror sight you could, of course, just open the cover all the way until it is even with the base plate and use it like a simple plate compass. But that's not using such a compass to full advantage. A better method is to open the cover part way and, holding the compass in your left hand (if you're right-handed), aim it approximately at the target by looking at the V-sight with one eye. Adjust the cover so that you can see the capsule in the mirror. That means holding the compass at about eye level; a little higher for a target higher than your location, somewhat lower for the target below you.

Step 2. Box the needle by turning the capsule (presumably with your right hand) while aiming your compass at the target.

With the mirror compass the black line in the mirror must run through the center of the compass and the index mark (see Figure 7.14).

Step 3. Walk, snowshoe, ski, or whatever to your destination—without reading the degree scale at all—simply by keeping the needle boxed.

It's awkward to walk with a compass in your hand, and nearly impossible to ski or snowshoe. So point your compass ahead, with the needle boxed, and look for a landmark such as a rock or a prominent tree. Then walk, ski, or snowshoe toward that landmark. When you get there repeat the process and find yourself another intermediate mark.

With a mirror compass you look through your V-sight with the needle boxed and the black line in the mirror running through the center of the compass until you locate a landmark on the course to your target. Repeat the process when you get there.

Such intermediate marks serve us well. Suppose you come to a stream without a bridge. Find a mark on your line of position on the other side of the stream. Then go upstream or downstream until you find a bridge or ford. Once across the stream, just walk to your mark. When you reach it, resume your course as if you had never deviated from it.

My instruction above, "without reading the degree scale at all," may have bothered some people. Suppose you decide to give up on the steep climb and return to your car parked in Milner Pass. How can you make a 180° turn when you don't know what your original course was?

That's easy. Walk in the direction opposite to the one the direction-of-travel arrow points. The easiest way to do this is to box the South end of the needle rather than the North end for the return trip.

If you followed this problem—admittedly not the most common one—you'll be surprised how many parts of it you'll use in the problems that follow.

Walking a Given Course

In the last example, if you had read the dial you would have got about 140°. Now suppose a friend invites you to use his cabin. He tells you exactly where to park your car. "And from there," he says, "you walk about one mile, 140° by compass. You won't see the cabin until you are almost there."

The problem is obviously similar to the last one; and again you don't need a map.

Step 1. Turn the capsule to set the course—140°—at the index mark. That'll be at the base of the direction-of-travel arrow on a simple compass, near the center of the mirror hinge on a mirror-sight model.

Step 2. With the compass in your hand, turn your whole body, feet included, to box the needle. If you didn't cheat by just twisting your hips or your wrist, your feet now face the destination.

With a mirror sight you can't cheat. Turn your body, again feet and all, until you have boxed the needle with the black line through the middle. What you see in the V of the sight is your first landmark.

Step 3. Walk, ski, or snowshoe in the direction you are facing, keeping the needle boxed. Or better yet, find yourself landmarks, one after the other, until you reach the cabin.

A practical application of that technique might be found in guidebooks: "A spring is located ¼ mile distant, bearing 140° from the peak." People who don't know how to walk a given course go thirsty.

Orienting the Map

This is the simplest example of using map and compass together. It means positioning the map so that it matches what you see. Since maps have North on top, you turn the map with the aid of a compass so that its top edge is facing North.

If your scenery and map include Half Dome, Mount Rushmore, or the Matterhorn, you simply turn the map by what you see. If any of these mountains are lined up with the map, everything on the map is lined up with the real world.

But what do you do when there are no recognizable features around, say in the Florida Everglades?

Step 1. Turn the capsule until 0° (360° or simply N on some models) is at the index mark, which you'll recall is at the base of the direction-of-travel arrow, or at the middle of the hinge on the mirror-sight models.

Step 2. Place the compass with the travel arrow pointing toward the top of the map along the left or right margin of the map.

Step 3. Turn map and compass together until the needle is boxed. Now North on the map and North in the landscape are in the same direction. And so, of course, are all other directions. (Figure 7.3)

With protractor compasses, orienting a map is seldom necessary. You most likely will use the technique to identify the peaks, lakes, and villages you see from some lookout point.

Your hiking map may not take in enough territory to identify distant features; you may need a map on a scale such as 1:250,000, which in the latitude covered by our map takes in about 70 by 110 statute miles (110 by 170 kilometers).

Finding a Course from the Map

This is probably the most often used map-and-compass operation. Each step is illustrated in Figures 7.4 through 7.9.

Step 1. Place one of the back corners of your compass on your starting position on the map. Turn the compass until the same edge is on your destination. If you start with a back corner, the direction-of-travel arrow automatically points in the right direction.

On a 1:24,000 scale map that'll work if the two points are no more than a mile or two apart. In the mountains you can rarely walk even that far in a straight line. But in the desert your compass is just too short to reach a destination more than one hour's walk away. Even the open cover of a mirror-sight model doesn't make it long enough.

You probably guessed: in this situation you can lay your ruler from start to destination then place the compass alongside the ruler, making sure the direction of travel arrow points toward the destination.

Step 2. Turn the capsule—with the boxing mark upward—to align its lines with the left or right margin of the map. Disregard the compass needle at this stage.

You can align the capsule by eye alone as you did in the preliminary practice at the beginning of this chapter, or with nearby survey lines. For greater accuracy slide the compass along the ruler to one of the vertical

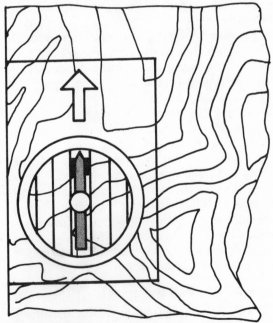

Figure 7.3 *Orienting the map.*

margins of the map and align the meridians with that.

The first two course-finding operations require only a map and compass and could have been performed indoors. Now you have to step out into the landscape or, to use a shorter term, the *field*.

Step 3. With the compass in your hand turn your body (feet and all) until the compass needle gets into the box. The direction of travel arrow, or the wide open cover of a mirror compass, now points toward your destination.

For greater accuracy using a mirror-sight compass, box the needle (with the black line through the center of the needle and the index mark), then look up through the V of the sight directly at your target.

Any prominent object in the sight, or in line with the direction of travel arrow on the simpler compasses, is your intermediate landmark.

Sometimes you get lucky: some distant object beyond your destination happens to be exactly in line with it. You may be aiming to reach a saddle with a peak behind it that happens to be in exactly the same direction. In these rare cases—which are often easily verified on the map, by laying your ruler from your position across the saddle to the peak, for example—you might as well put away your compass and walk toward the distant landmark using only your eyes.

A small warning: it's tempting to use a star or planet, which looks just like a star, as a distant landmark when walking at night, say in the desert to take advantage of the coolness. But the stars don't stand still. How fast they drift, and even in which direction in some parts of the sky, isn't easy to figure out. Best advice: enjoy your walk toward a star (or planet), but after ten minutes check with your compass. You may have to walk a bit to the left (or sometimes right) of your star. Check again after ten minutes. Eventually you'll find a new star to guide you.

Finding a Mapped Object

This problem is closely related to finding a course. When you know where you are, consider that as the starting point, the mapped object as the destination. Work out the course as described above.

When you have the needle boxed you are looking straight at the feature you want to find—a peak, lake, saddle, or whatever. With the mirror-sight compass you can actually put the object you want to find in your sight.

Identifying a Mapped Object

From a known position you see an object so prominent you can assume it will be found on your topo map.

What looks like a small pond may be just the remains of the last snow to melt and will be gone in a week; it will not be mapped. But a good-sized lake is certain to be mapped.

Say you want to know what peak it is over there that you can see from the peak you're standing on.

In the last two problems we asked: "What course must I walk, or in what direction must I aim the compass to hit that destination or mapped object?" Here the question is: "If I walked (or aimed my compass) in that direction, what feature on the map would I reach?" Each step is illustrated in Figures 7.10 through 7.15.

Step 1. Start by taking a sight; that is, point the direction-of-travel arrow in a simple plate compass, or use V-sight and mirror as before.

Step 2. Turn the capsule to box the needle.

Step 3. Place one rear corner of your compass on your position on the map, and turn the entire compass—not the capsule—so that the lines in the capsule run parallel to the vertical map margins, as always with the boxing mark on top.

The edge of your compass you used for your position in the course-finding problem now points—in the direction-of-travel arrow—toward the object to be identified. If the compass is too short, use your ruler along that edge to make it longer.

When there is a possibility of confusion with a nearby similar object, say another peak close to the one you want to identify, use your ruler for aligning the compass from the map margin. Usually there's no worry and the extra accuracy is not needed.

For example, you and your party have just reached the point in section 12 of our map where the Red Mountain trail meets the Grand Ditch. Your son asks, "What's the name of the mountain over there?"

You hand him your map and compass and instruct him as above.

When he puts the compass on the map and turns it to make the lines in the capsule parallel to the vertical edges of the map, there is no doubt: he was looking at Shipler Mountain. And you have another compass expert in your family.

The next problem is closely related to this one.

Getting a Position Line from a Known Object

Here we know where the mapped object is but don't know our position.

For example, where are you when walking along the Grand Ditch you measure the bearing of the more northerly peak of Shipler Mountain as 83°?

In the last example it mattered little which peak your son sighted on. A simple plate compass was all that was needed. Even if he had been a couple of degrees off in setting the capsule lines parallel with the map margins, it wouldn't have mattered. He would still have got Shipler Mountain and no other for his answer.

But for getting your position from a bearing, the greater the accuracy the closer to the real position you will be.

A compass with a mirror sight, properly handled, is highly recommended for this type of problem. And don't align the capsule by eye only; use the ruler and the map margin.

The technique for taking the bearing, also called the azimuth, is the same as before:

Step 1. Aim a simple baseplate compass, or get the target in the V-sight of a mirror model.

Step 2. Turn the capsule to box the needle.

Now the instructions have to differ. You don't know your position, so you can't place a rear corner of the compass on it. Instead, do this:

Step 3. Place a *front* corner of your compass on the known object on the map.

Step 4. Turn the entire compass—not the capsule—so that the lines in the capsule run parallel to the vertical map margin. (In this example you have a range line conveniently located right under your capsule.)

The edge of your compass you have used for getting a course is now along your position line. If the compass is too short to reach your position, use the ruler. You'll find you are near the bench mark 10,241.

Don't let the direction-of-travel arrow mislead you. As in the last problem, your position is near the rear of the compass on the map, just like the starting position when you are finding a course.

The *bearing* of Shipler Mountain here is the *course* a bird starting from your position would fly to reach the northerly peak.

You already know that you didn't need a road or a trail to fix your position. You could have done that from two bearings. As you can guess, finding your position from two bearings is the mainstay of navigation in cross-country travel.

Summary

In this chapter I have tried to show how walking a field bearing or a given course, finding a course from the map, finding or identifying a mapped object, and getting a position line from a bearing are all variations of the same basic operations. At first you may feel that I've tried to present too much information at once. Other books skip many of these routines or present each as a separate routine to be memorized. In the long run I think you will understand them better if you can see how they are related.

Perhaps I can make your practical work easier by pointing out this:

On the *map* you always work with the *lines* of the capsule;

In the *field* you always work with the compass *needle*.

The following illustrations will help you visualize the most important routines. The drawings and cap-

tions can also serve as a quick review when you have
gone hazy between trips.

Basic Procedure for Finding a Course

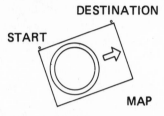

Figure 7.4 *Lay a rear corner of the compass on your starting point on
the map, one long edge pointing to your destination. Ignore capsule and
needle. Double check: arrow must point toward destination.*

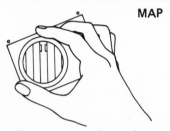

Figure 7.5 *Hold the compass in place on the map. Turn the capsule until
the gate is up and lines are parallel with left or right map margin. Ignore
needle. Double check: gate must be up.*

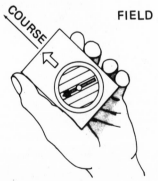

Figure 7.6 *Holding the compass in front of you, turn your entire body
until the needle is boxed in the gate. You and the arrow now face your
destination. Double check: the needle's North end must be in the gate.*

More Accurate Procedure for Finding a Course

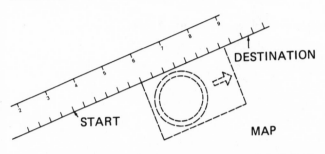

Figure 7.7 *Align a ruler between the starting point and the destination. Lay the compass with one long edge alongside the ruler with the arrow pointing toward the destination. Ignore the capsule and needle. Double check: the arrow must point toward the destination.*

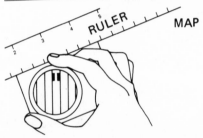

Figure 7.8 *Holding the ruler and compass steady, turn the capsule to bring the gate upward. Slide the compass along the ruler to map margin for accurate alignment of lines. Ignore the needle. Double check: the gate must be up.*

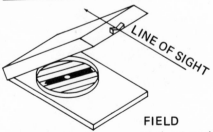

Figure 7.9 *Use the compass with the mirror sight. Holding the compass at eye level, turn your body until the needle is boxed. Line of sight now points at the destination. Double check: the needle's North end must be in the gate.*

Basic Procedure for Taking a Bearing

FIELD

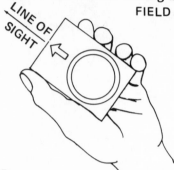

Figure 7.10 *Aim the direction-of-travel arrow at a mapped target. Ignore capsule and needle. Double check: the arrow must point at the target.*

FIELD

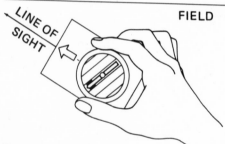

Figure 7.11 *While aiming the compass at the target, turn the capsule until the needle is boxed. Double check: the needle's North end must be in the gate.*

MAP

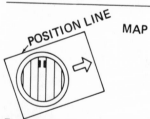

Figure 7.12 *Place the compass with gate upward on the map so that the known point, your position or a target, is on one long edge. Turn the entire compass to make the lines parallel to the left or right map margin. The edge in the direction of the arrow now points to the target, in the opposite direction to your position.*

More Accurate Procedure for Taking a Bearing

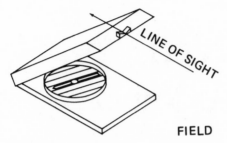

Figure 7.13 *Use the mirror sight. Aim at the mapped target. While keeping the object in sight, turn the capsule until the North end of the needle is boxed.*

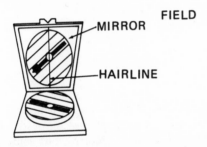

Figure 7.14 *With the target in the sight and the needle boxed, the hairline in the mirror must seem to pass through the exact center of the compass.*

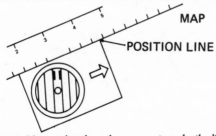

Figure 7.15 *Use a ruler along the compass to make the lines in the capsule, with gate up, parallel with left or right map margin, and to connect the known point—your position or target—and the unknown one. The direction-of-travel arrow points at your target; your position is in the opposite direction.*

8.
Magnetic Direction

You know that maps show true directions. You also already know that in most places compasses don't point to true North (geographic North), but somewhat off to one side or the other. *Declination* is the angle between true North and magnetic North. Sailors call it *variation*.

In the contiguous United States the declination varies from 20° West of true North in the Northeast (Maine) to 21° East of true North in the Northwest (Washington). In either place, if you ignored the declination you'd be about 2000 feet off for every mile traveled (350 meters for every kilometer). And every bearing you took would be off by the same distance for every mile or kilometer between you and your target.

To help you remember: that error works out to 100 feet per degree per mile. In metric units it is—not quite so neatly—18 meters per degree per kilometer.

You may have learned in elementary school that a compass needle points to the magnetic North Pole,

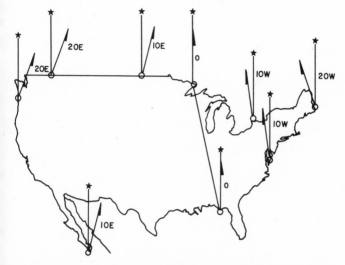

Figure 8.1 *Declination at selected U.S. locations. Line with star indicates true North; line with arrow indicates the direction of the compass needle at each location (magnetic North). The angle between the two is the declination.*

which is some distance from the geographic North Pole. The geographic North Pole, from which all meridians radiate, gives the direction of true North anywhere on earth.

You may also have come across a map of the United States that tried to show the difference between true North and the direction of a compass needle by a series of lines.

One line, marked zero—connecting the Great Lakes and Florida—is known as the *agonic* (no-angle) line. Along that line the declination is zero, there is no angle between true and magnetic North. The other lines, connecting places where the angle is the same, are known as *isogonic* lines, or simply isogonics.

A casual glance shows that the eastern lines are labeled WEST; the ones west of the agonic line are labeled EAST. All converge toward the top of the map. But, contrary to what you have been taught, they don't run directly toward magnetic North.

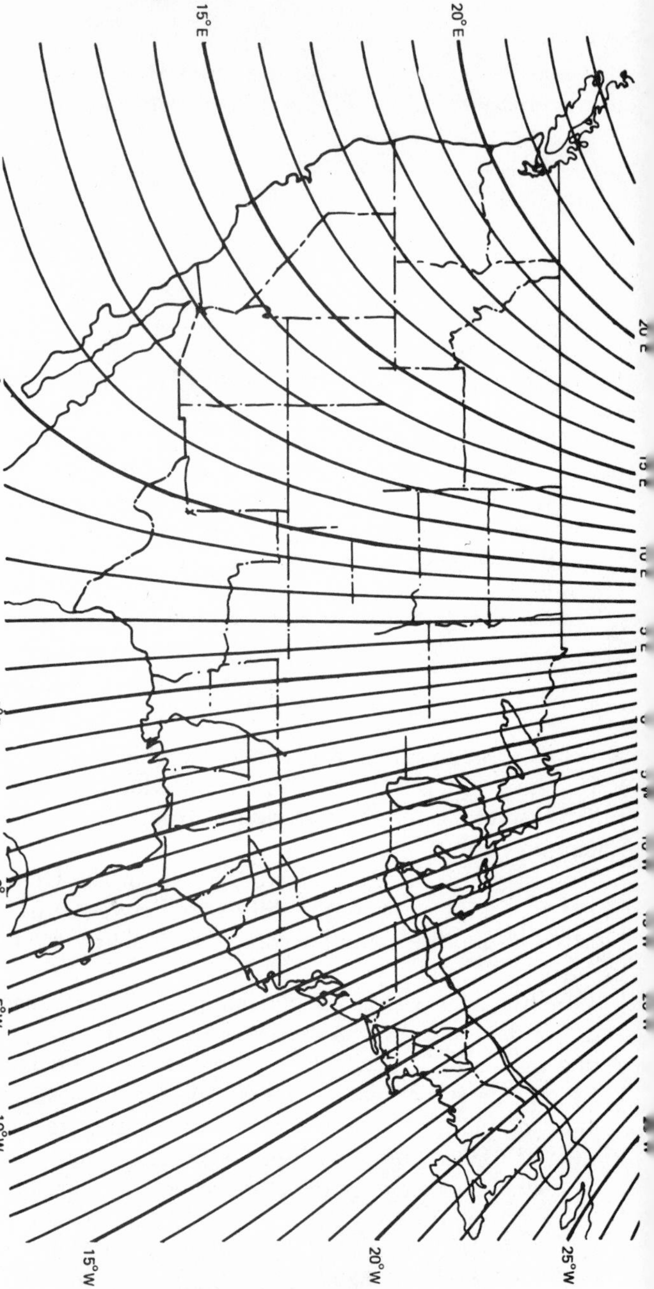

Figure 8.2 *Declination (1980.0) in the United States.*

Almost everything you have learned about this subject is grossly misleading, if not downright false. The only fact I won't argue with is that the magnetic North Pole is some distance from the geographic pole.

Contrary to what teachers and instruction sheets may tell you, compass needles do *not* point to the magnetic North Pole. And the relation between the two poles has little to do with the declination of a given place.

The magnetic North Pole moves slowly; in 1980, the date of the map shown in Figure 8.2, it was near longitude 104°W. Since that's where the two poles are in line, the agonic line should follow that meridian. The line of zero declination should pass near Cheyenne, Wyoming, and Carlsbad, New Mexico, instead of Chicago, Illinois and Tallahassee, Florida.

Nowhere does the agonic line follow that meridian. In the Americas it steers a course of about 15° East of South at first, gradually increasing that angle to 25°. No point of South America is within a thousand miles of the 104th meridian. But the agonic line enters that continent near Panama, and leaves it near Bahia Blanca, Argentina, at longitude 62°W! (That's about 2300 miles (3600 kilometers) from the meridian that connects the magnetic and geographic poles.)

If the magnetic poles were as well behaved as the bar magnets you experimented with at school the magnetic South Pole would come out exactly opposite the magnetic North Pole; that is, near latitude 79°S and longitude 76°E. Actually, in 1980, the magnetic South Pole was near latitude 65°S and longitude 139°E.

But even that does not explain the strangeness of the earth's magnetic field. If it did, the isogonic lines, including the agonic line, would form a neat geometric pattern on a globe.

The agonic line through North and South America about which you just read is a model of conformity compared to its other arm, which enters Europe on a civilized southerly course in Scandinavia and leaves it in Sicily. It swings through Libya, the Sudan, and Ethiopia then veers toward Karachi and New Delhi. It then turns through China and Mongolia, then almost due North through Russia into the Arctic Ocean, then loops back South through the Philippines, West to Vietnam, and across to Sumatra and westernmost Australia to the magnetic South Pole.

You don't need to dust off your globe to see that this is not a line dictated by the position of the geographic or magnetic poles.

Other isogonic lines are no better behaved. A gaggle of them form a closed pattern around Verkhoyansk in northeastern Siberia, like the isobars of a gigantic high pressure area.

Fortunately there's a rather simple conclusion to all this for readers in the United States and Canada. Once you know, however roughly, where the agonic line runs across the continent, you'll always have a check on whether the declination is East or West. In the White Mountains and the Laurentians it must be West; in the Rockies, in the United States and Canada, it's East.

Change in Declination

Anyone who wants to can find the declination for any particular location in the United States in a number of books. Recently even some instruction sheets for compasses include isogonic maps.

When I last saw the area of our map, in 1977, we used a map published in 1958, when the declination there was 15°E. That year the map was photorevised and the declination updated to 13°E. In 1982 it was down to 12°E.

From the map shown in Figure 8.3 you can see that at present the change in the contiguous 48 states varies from a minimum of 5' E or W per year (meaning it'll take 12 years to change the declination by one degree) to a maximum of 12'W (meaning it changes one degree in five years).

Hawaii, where the declination is 11°E to 12°E, has virtually no annual change now.

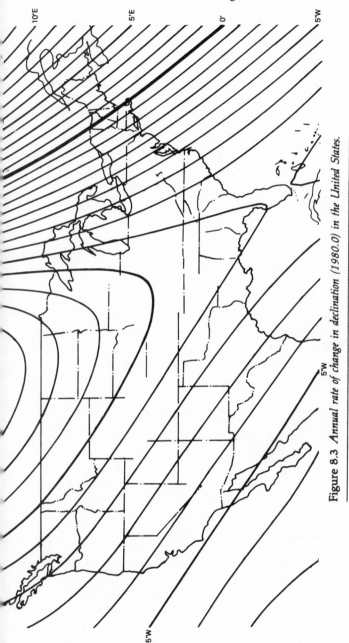

Figure 8.3 *Annual rate of change in declination (1980.0) in the United States.*

Table 8.1 Change in declination at London, England, since 1600

Year	Declination	Mean change*
1600	8°E	8'W
1650	1°E	10'W
1700	7°W	13'W
1750	18°W	7'W
1800	24°W	2'E
1850	22°W	7'E
1900	16°W	10'E
1950	8°W	4'E
1980	6°W	

* per year

In Alaska the declination is easterly—35°E at the eastern border, virtually zero in the most westerly Aleutian Islands. Alaska's annual change in declination now falls between 5'E and 5'W.

You may have wondered why a repeat of "at present" and "now." I want to warn you that the declination change itself changes in time (see Table 8.1). London is often used as an example of this phenomenon, probably because of the accurate records available there. Note that not only has the magnitude of declination changed, but also the direction.

Enough. What you want to know is: how can I find the declination where it interests me and for this year?

Declination from Map and Compass

Perhaps surprisingly, the most accurate method for finding local declination is finding it yourself. That's not only my opinion; the U.S. Geological Survey people, who should know, state that "there is no better way to obtain the magnetic declination; anything else published is an approximation of this method." All you need is a detailed map, on a scale of say 1:24,000, 1:25,000, 1:50,000, or 1:62,500, and a compass.

If you use a compass that you just point for taking bearings, don't bother with this method. But without any knowledge of local declination, you can get at least an idea of its magnitude and direction even with such a simple compass.

One recommended procedure has you orient your map along a mapped straight line—a road, railroad, telephone line, or pipeline. To orient a map, you'll recall, means making the upper edge of the map face true North.

First you use your compass to get approximate North. When the image on the map is parallel to the straight line in the landscape, the map is oriented.

Cautions: I don't have to warn you about spreading your map on a turnpike. On country roads, a power-line or telephone line close by may affect your compass.

Railroad tracks, unless stripped of rails and wires, and pipelines are also likely to deflect your compass. The trick then is to work parallel to, rather than right on top of, these reference lines.

When you have the map oriented by the straight line, place your compass (travel arrow facing North) with one of its long edges along the right or left margin of the map, and box the needle.

If the declination is West you can read it directly off the degree scale on your compass. For example, when you read 10°, the declination here and now is 10°W. When you read a figure somewhat below 360°, such as 350°, subtract it from 360° and label it East; in this case, 10°E.

I used that method on a recent hiking trip in Austria. Only at the trailhead did I discover that my map, unlike U.S. topo maps, gave no hint of the local declination. It could have been 1° or 20°, East or West. I sighted along one cable of a chairlift shown on the map. (To avoid the magnetic disturbance of the cables and machinery I stood in the empty parking lot.) That bearing gave a neglible declination; exactly right as I found out later.

Another method requires two known, mapped points rather than a straight line. In the mountains pairs of such points are easier to find than straight lines. And they won't distract your compass.

When you have found the two points—say the trail crossing where you are and an unmistakable peak—on the map, work out the course from where you are to the other point. Work as accurately as you can, using the ruler as described in Chapter 7.

Then take the bearing of the second point. Say you get a bearing of 55°, and the course came out as 45°. The difference between the (true) course and the (magnetic) bearing is 10°. Label the difference—the local declination—West when the bearing is greater than the course, as in this example. If the numbers were switched, you'd label it East.

If your compass has an adjustment to allow for declination, it must be set to zero while you work out what the declination is, unless you just want to check that you have set it right.

Declination from Polaris

Polaris, the North Star, gives another check on declination. For this method you don't need a map and don't have to know your position.

Most people in the northern hemisphere know how to find Polaris from the Big Dipper. And from Polaris, on any clear night, you can get North. The Big Dipper method of finding Polaris is illustrated in Figure 11.2.

Look at the northern sky. There, as many degrees above the horizon as you are North of the equator, you will find Polaris. If you're near latitude 40°N, it will be 40° above the horizon. With your arm outstretched, a spread hand from thumb to little finger measures about 20° in the sky; a fist, thumb showing, covers 10°; each finger, about 2°. So in latitude 40°N Polaris will be about two spread hands above the horizon. It is a second-magnitude star, which means it remains visible even when the moon is full.

Polaris is about midway between the Big Dipper's guide stars and the constellation Cassiopeia. That's the one that looks to some people like a chair, to most of us like a sloppy capital letter M or W, depending on which side is up.

So now you have three ways to find or check on Polaris. There is no equally bright or brighter star nearby to confuse you. (Planets don't get to that part of the sky.)

Polaris is such a good guide for finding true North that surveyors use it routinely, every day. Yes, day. In their telescopes it's visible in broad daylight.

Of course, surveyors need more accuracy than we do, so they carry a table that gives a correction for the time of observation. But South of latitude 40°N Polaris is always within one degree of true North. Between that latitude and the Arctic Circle it is always within two degrees.

You can eliminate most of these errors. Consider Polaris as the center of a clock face. It is due North when the bowl of the Big Dipper is between twelve and one o'clock or between six and seven o'clock; or when Cassiopeia is between seven and eight o'clock or between one and two o'clock.

It's probably good enough to remember that Polaris is due North when either Cassiopeia or the bowl of the Big Dipper is either above or below it.

Polaris is at its greatest distance from true North six hours after these configurations.

Polaris is on the Cassiopeia side of true North. So when Cassiopeia is right (East) of Polaris, Polaris is East of North; when Cassiopeia is left (West) of Polaris, Polaris is West of North. If you prefer, you can remember that Polaris is on the opposite side of true North from the Big Dipper.

If you are planning to use Polaris for getting compass declination, the times of least error may be helpful. They are listed in Table 8.2.

I'm well aware that it may not be dark enough to see Polaris at some of these times in some latitudes.

But within two hours before and after the times given, Polaris will be within one degree of true North and on the Cassiopeia side right up to the Arctic Circle.

Declination from the Sun

There is a method for getting the declination whenever the sun shines at noon. The main tool is a level surface the size of your compass. That may be hard to find on the trail, but an outdoor table in the valley will do the trick.

The method is based on the fact that by definition the sun in our part of the northern hemisphere is due South—casting its shadow due North—at local noon. Local time, on which sun and earth operate, only accidentally coincides with the time we live by, standard or daylight saving time.

Table 11.3 and instructions in Chapter 11 let you calculate local noon to the nearest minute. That's how accurate you have to be to get the declination to a useful one-degree error.

I assume you can get accurate time from radio, tele-

Table 8.2 Times of least error for locating true North with the aid of Polaris

Month	Time of least error
Jan.	7 A.M. and P.M.
Feb.	5 A.M. and P.M.
Mar.	3 A.M.
Apr.	1 A.M.
May	11 P.M.
June	9 P.M.
July	7 A.M. and P.M.
Aug.	5 A.M.
Sept.	3 A.M.
Oct.	1 A.M.
Nov.	11 P.M.
Dec.	9 A.M. and P.M.

vision (network programs in the United States start on
the dot), a Western Union office, to check your wristwatch. Many wristwatches, even moderately priced
ones, now let you carry accurate time into the wilderness and can be trusted to keep accurate time for several days. Check yours before your trip.

The practical measurement of the declination is easiest if you have a compass with a mirror sight. We
won't use the mirror, though; the sun is too bright for
that and could damage your eyes, even with sunglasses.

We'll use the cover's shadow only. Open the cover
part way and turn the entire compass so that the
shadow falls along the long edges of the compass,
which must be resting on a horizontal surface. (The
lower the cover, the longer the shadow.)

The shadow is best seen on a light surface, say a
white paper underneath your compass. Start your experiment a few minutes before calculated local noon.

Look at both edges of your compass; once you have
it about right, concentrate on the left edge, where the
shadow creeps out. When the actual minute of noon
arrives, all you need to do is correct the position of the
compass ever so slightly.

If a thick cloud just killed all shadows, have another
beer and come back tomorrow.

But if you see the compass sitting on its shadow,
box the needle without moving the compass. If there's
no declination where you perform your magic, the dial
will read 180°. If it reads 190°, you have measured the
declination as 10°W; if it reads 170°, the declination is
10°E.

With a plain base plate compass, without a cover to
cast a shadow, you'll have to find some vertical edge
(for example, a box or fuel bottle) to cast the shadow.

Anywhere North of latitude 37°N the azimuth of the
sun, timed to the minute, is accurate within one degree
all year round. South of that latitude and right to the
edge of the tropics it is equally accurate from the end
of August to mid-April. At latitude 30°N it is within
two degrees, at worst, around the summer solstice, but
the accuracy deteriorates rapidly South of there.

If you find yourself in the southern hemisphere, where the sun bears North at noon, the dial will read 360° where the declination is zero. If it reads 10°, you have measured a declination of 10°W; if it reads 350°, 10°E.

South of latitude 37°S the azimuth of the sun at local noon, timed to the minute, is accurate within one degree all year round. North of that latitude and right to the edge of the tropics it is equally accurate from the end of February to mid-October. At latitude 30°S it is within two degrees, at worst (around Christmas), but the accuracy deteriorates rapidly north of there.

In the tropics this method is useless.

Declination from the Map

After finding declination on the spot by one of the above methods, the next best method is to rely on maps.

The master map is called simply *Magnetic Variation* (you'll recall that variation is the nautical term for declination) and covers most of the world (from latitude 70°S to latitude 84°N). It is prepared and published by the Defense Mapping Agency Hydrographic/Topographic Center, Washington, D.C. 20315 as map number 42. (The remaining parts of the world are covered in map number 43.)

That's enough information to order it from any chart agent (chart is nautical for map). Since there are few inland chart agents you could send $4 to the above address and ask for stock number WOBZC 42.

This chart or map is updated every five years; the latest available is marked Epoch 1980.0, which translates as the beginning of that year.

The map shows declination lines at one-degree intervals—every fifth isogonic line printed heavier—in purple ink superimposed on a map of the world on a scale of 1:39,000,000 at the equator. It is drawn on the Mercator projection (straight parallels of latitude and straight meridians), in which the scale varies with latitude.

Nowhere except near the magnetic poles are the isogonic lines more closely spaced than in the eastern United States. But for our purposes they are still far enough apart.

The annual change in declination, at one-minute intervals, is printed on the same map in blue ink.

To get the current declination for any area, you first find it on the map. (An atlas may help you pinpoint your area of interest.) Then follow the nearest purple lines to where they are labeled. I would note the declination to the nearest half degree.

Close to 10°W I'd call it 10°W; close to 11°W, 11°W; and near the middle of the interval, 10½°W.

Next identify the magnitude and direction of the change from the nearest blue line. Multiply that change by the number of years elapsed since the epoch of the map. At the beginning of 1984, four years after the epoch, you'd multiply by 4; in July of that year 4½ would be the more accurate figure. Say the change was 6' a year. That makes the change in July 1984 roughly half a degree.

If the declination is West and the change is also West, or when both are East, you add declination and change. If one is West, and the other is East, you subtract the change.

Let's say the change was 6'W. If you add that change over 4½ years to a declination of 10½°W, in mid-1984 it would be 11°W.

Had the change in declination been 6'E per year, the mid-1984 declination would be 10°.

If you have difficulty with the rule for adding or subtracting, try this: think not of declination but of distance. You are 10½ miles West of your camp. Walking ½ mile West gets you 11 miles from your camp. If you walked ½ mile East, you'd end up 10 miles from camp. (Work it out yourself where you'd be if you started 10½ miles East of your camp.)

The declination and change-of-declination maps in this chapter are based on map number 42. If they cover where you want to go you can safely use them until 1985 and a few years beyond.

If your interest is only for the United States, order U.S. Geological Survey chart I-1283 from one of the

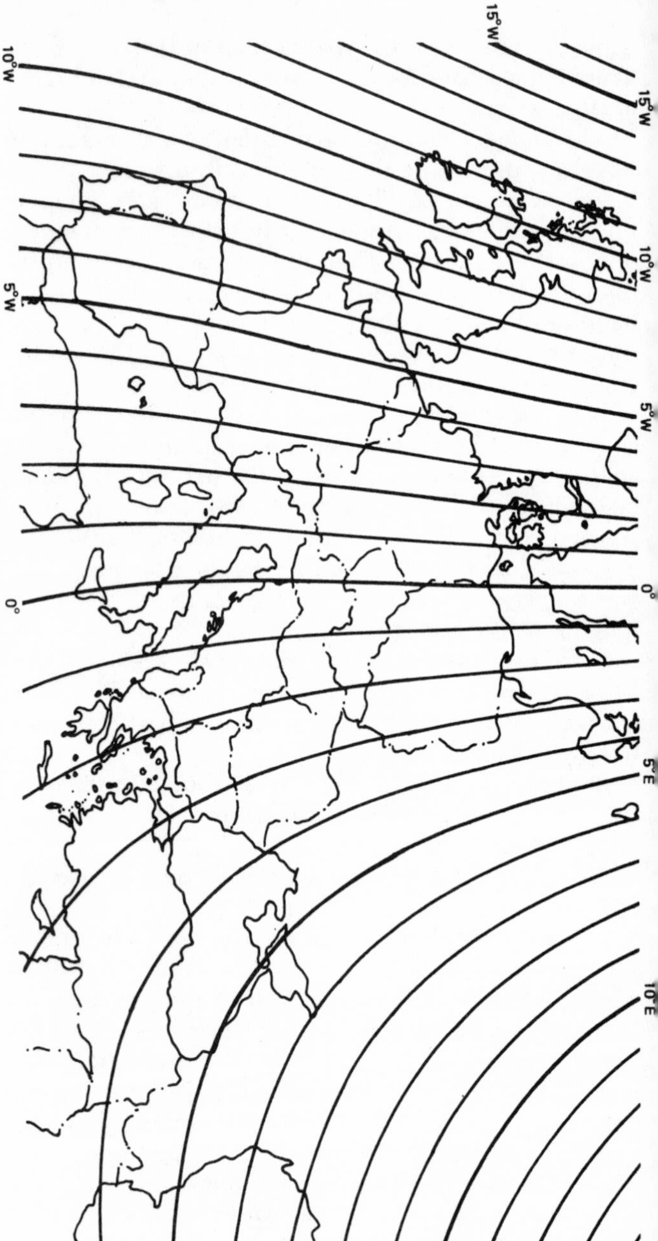

Figure 8.4 *Declination (1980.0) in Europe.*

addresses given in Chapter 2. The same chapter gives the address for ordering the corresponding map for Canada.

Even if you never use these maps, don't rely on any published map without applying the change in declination.

The makers of a new compass thoughtfully provide a map of declination in the United States in the instruction booklet. I checked three points, one each in northern Maine, Florida, and northwestern Washington. Before my compass arrived, the isogonic lines at all three points were already one degree off.

You can practice finding declination for any year to 1985 with the maps of Europe provided in Figures 8.4 and 8.5.

Topo map users in the United States, if they are aware of declination, rely on the diagram printed on the popular 7½' and 15' maps (Figure 8.6).

The diagram, an elaboration of an earlier design, gives the declination in figures (to the nearest half degree) and shows the direction in which the magnetic needle (MN) of a compass points in relation to true North, which is always given straight up and is indicated by a line ending in a star.

Here are several warnings from the U.S. Geological Survey on the use of this diagram:

1. The angle between the lines gives the direction (here East) of the declination, not necessarily the correct number of degrees. You get those from the printed number.
2. The value is for the year given and will have changed since then.
3. The declination given refers to the center of the sheet. This has little importance for outdoor sports and travel. Where the lines are closest, in the eastern United States, the declination changes at most by one degree in 50 miles. So on any of these topographic quads the value is virtually the same anywhere on the map.
4. There might be some local magnetic attraction. It's not terribly likely that you'll be misled by

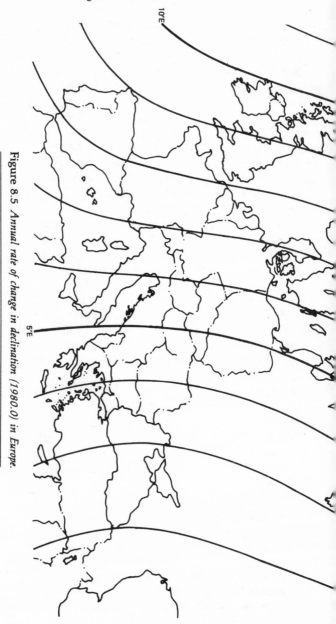

Figure 8.5 Annual rate of change in declination (1980.0) in Europe.

UTM GRID AND 1977 MAGNETIC NORTH
DECLINATION AT CENTER OF SHEET

Figure 8.6 *Declination diagram.*

that phenomenon. Put differently, you are not too
likely to discover an iron or nickel mine with
your base plate compass.

Grid North (GN) is of little interest to outdoors people, but interests surveyors. It refers to the direction of
meridians on maps that take in much more territory
than our topo maps (4° latitude by 6° longitude on a
scale of 1:1,000,000). Our map is in Zone 13 of that series of maps; that zone stretches from longitude 102°W
to longitude 108°W. Its central meridian (105°W) is
drawn running due North, and all other meridians of
that zone are drawn parallel to it.

The central meridian of the sheet from which our
map is cut (105°48'45"W) is drawn pointing due North.
Since meridians converge toward the pole, that meridian must make a small angle with the grid of the Universal Transverse Mercator Map of Zone 13. That's the
angle referred to in the figure, 0°32'.

The left and right margins of the map, which we
used for aligning the meridian lines in the compass
capsule, are also true meridians. That is, they run to
true North exactly. As a result our topo quads are a
trifle narrower at the top than at the bottom. The difference is not noticeable until you put the top and bottom edges together.

For our purposes, we could use the declination from
the diagram (13°E) corrected for the yearly change

(from Figure 8.3) multiplied by the number of years since 1977 (the year for which the topo quad gives the declination).

For example, in 1982, five years after the date on the map, the correction is close to 1°, to be subtracted because it is West, while the declination is East. You won't be far off if you carry the same annual change a few years past the official replacement date in 1985.

9.

Allowing for Declination

Say you know what the declination is in your area of operation. What do you do with that information?

You have four choices:

1. You can ignore it—sometimes.
2. If your compass has an adjustment for declination, set it and and forget about it until you move on to an area with different declination.
3. Draw lines on your map and use them in place of the map margins to align the lines in your compass capsule. I'll show you a fast, accurate way of doing this that's less work than the usual method.
4. You can add the declination to or subtract it from the figures shown on the 360° scale of your compass. The rules about when to add and when to subtract are easy to learn, but just as easy to mix up.

Ignoring Declination

In a few operations you can ignore the declination, however large it may be.

Walking a field bearing, for example. Whatever correction you should apply to the bearing is cancelled by the correction to be applied to the course to be walked.

There are a few operations in which a small error hardly matters. Orienting a map for example. Once you have it approximately lined up for North on top, you can spot some prominent object. You then ignore any small error and adjust by a tug at the corner of the map rather than by compass work.

Finding a mapped mountain peak in the landscape or identifying one on the map are similar to orienting the map and require only low accuracy.

Deciding which fork in a road or trail to take doesn't need high accuracy. And probably nobody would worry about declination for stringing a laundry line to catch the morning sun.

I may get an argument from some experts, but I believe the question of ignoring declination or correcting for it depends somewhat on your compass. If by chance you use one of the optical sighting compasses that reads reliably to one half of one degree, you'd be silly to ignore declination, even if it's only a degree or so. But with a simpler compass you might feel silly correcting for one degree declination.

Bearings taken for fixing your position require the greatest accuracy and if taken with a mirror type compass should be corrected even for minimal declination.

The use of declination also depends on the terrain. For example, a rough course will get you close enough to a lake to see it and correct your course. You may want to be more accurate when you're trying to reach the only bridge over a ravine or a single ford through a stream. (Chapter 13 describes a useful trick for such situations.) And when dragging yourself to your water cache in the desert, you'll want all the accuracy you can squeeze out of your compass.

Even the weather may influence your choice of ignoring the declination or correcting for it. For example, what was a well-beaten trail yesterday has been obliterated by snow. Blazes and color markings are hard to spot. Even cairns—called ducks or stonemen by some—are hiding. To add to the fun you can expect a whiteout at any time. Obviously, accurate compass work will be essential.

Mechanical Adjustment

The easiest way to correct for declination is to use a compass that lets you set the declination and forget it. That feature adds a few dollars to the cost of the compass, but the peace of mind may be worth it to you.

If you are in charge of a group, have the others struggle with arithmetic. With your model you'll never be wrong even while your mind is on other matters.

The mechanism for making the adjustment is similar in all the compasses I have checked. You offset the boxing mark—the orienting arrow, gate, slot, or whatever device is used for boxing the needle.

After adjustment the boxed compass needle does not run parallel to the orienting lines in the capsule but makes an angle with them toward either the East or the West.

That's achieved by a double bottom. A clearly marked scale lets you shift the boxing mark in relation to the capsule lines for exactly the amount and direction of the declination.

As explained in Chapter 6, the offset can be controlled by a miniature screwdriver, a small stud, a handle, or some other means, depending on the make of compass. The effect of all these mechanisms is the same. Some are easier on your fingers than others, but you won't change the adjustment all that often.

Don't forget to change it in an area of different declination. Perhaps you could make it a habit to see if it needs changing every time you break out a map. On adjoining sheets you probably won't have to do anything. But on the first map on a new trip you may be way off if you don't reset the compass adjustment.

Once the compass is set for the area of your activity, you can work all the routines described in Chapter 7 as if there were no such thing as declination.

Lining the Map

Another method often recommended for allowing for declination is to line the entire map with waterproof ink, inclining the lines at the angle and direction of the declination. These lines, called *magnetic meridians*, show how a compass needle would point in the map area (strictly speaking at the center of the map—a quibble—and certainly without interference from belt buckles, knives, transistor radios, and so on).

With these lines drawn on the map, you don't need rules or arithmetic. You use the magnetic meridians to align the meridians on the bottom of the capsule. And you don't have to move the compass along a ruler to the margin of the map. In other words, you use the magnetic meridians rather than geographic meridians. Otherwise the instructions remain the same.

This method makes compass use under stress foolproof (provided you keep the boxing mark in the capsule upward on the map), which is why maps for orienteering competitions are lined in this fashion.

To catch at least one line in the capsule, the drawn lines must be no more than 1 to 1½ inches (25 to 37 millimeters) apart. On the quad from which our map is taken, that means 18 lines up to 2 feet (60 centimeters) long must be drawn very accurately.

That's why I have observed that people who recommend this method don't use it themselves.

Most of us could handle the job on a nice flat table, perhaps with a borrowed T-square. But that's not always where we'd have to line the map. You buy some maps at the local hardware store, or perhaps have them sent to you general delivery at some country post office. Neither place is an ideal drafting room.

Some people recommend using the diagram on the topo map. But the United States Geological Survey, which produces these maps, specifically warns against that practice. The angles of the diagram merely show the relative directions of true, magnetic, and grid

North; therefore the angular values given *in figures* are to be used for corrections. Also, as you know, magnetic declination changes, so that the value on the map may be obsolete.

Even if the map you happen to be using shows an angle in the declination diagram that corresponds with the numerals and is so recent that the change in declination is small, using the diagram is still a poor method.

The arrow that points to magnetic North is 1 inch (25 millimeters) long. You are supposed to draw a line about 24 inches (60 centimeters) long. Bad enough in a drafting room. On location you probably have nothing longer than your 12-inch (30-centimeter) ruler. That means lining it up with the 1-inch arrow and drawing a 12-inch line; realigning it with the line just drawn and drawing another line; then repeating the second step to bring the line to the top of the map.

And that gives you just one line. With errors accumulating as you draw lines parallel to that line, accuracy will drop off some more. And when you have a stack of topo maps to line, you may be tempted to forget the whole procedure.

Some books recommend using your compass—set to the proper declination—in place of the diagram. Granted, the base of the compass is longer than the arrow in the diagram. But I don't think much of that method; a two-inch diameter scale, calibrated for every other degree, is not the proper protractor for drawing a line of that length.

The method described below for drawing these lines can be used in the coffee shop next to the store or post office where you picked up your map.

Our topo maps of the 7½' and 15' series are divided into thirds horizontally and vertically by ticks in all four margins and black crosses in the map area. (You can see one of the crosses on our map near the Northeast corner of section 7.) In other words, these maps are divided into nine quadrangles. Often you will know beforehand which of these areas you'll be in, which saves you ruling the entire map.

But that's a bonus. The real improvement gained by

making use of these quadrangles is in accuracy. And your longest line will be shorter than your ruler.

First you draw the third side of a triangle, one side of which is given by the vertical line between the map margin and a cross, or between two crosses. You look up the length of the second (horizontal) side in Table 9.1. Then measure the distance found there on a line from margin tick to cross or from cross to cross. You don't have to draw that line, just mark the end point.

When you mark that point, glance at the declination diagram on the map to see whether the triangle faces left or right. With two sides of the triangle determined, you simply draw in the third side to establish your first magnetic meridian.

Suppose you were to line the map from which our map is taken. It's a 7½′ quad, so you would use the

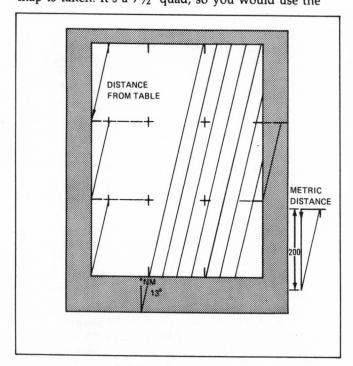

Figure 9.1 *Drawing magnetic meridians.*

first column in the table. In 1982 the declination in the
area was 12°E, for which Table 9.1 gives 41 millimeters.
The E tells you the line to be drawn must slope in
some northeasterly direction. The diagram makes that
very clear.

Say you start your lining in the bottom left ninth of
the map. Your line will start at the Southwest corner
of the map, and at the level of the first tick (25′) and
lowest cross it will be 41 millimeters to the right of the
left margin.

For westerly declination the triangle would face the
other way. For a 15′-series quad you would use the
second column in Table 9.1 and make the short side of
your triangle 32 millimeters long.

I leave it to you to work out how you measure the
next line and the next. One quick way is to make the
lines one ruler's width—probably 1¼ inch (32 millimeters)—apart.

For any map other than the 7½′ or 15′ series, of any
scale, you must make your own vertical side for the
triangle. Make it 200 millimeters long and use the third
column of Table 9.1.

Lining an entire map, or even only the parts you are
likely to need, is quite a bit of work. (You may not
mind it, since you saved the cost of the built-in adjustment in your compass.)

Here is a variation that is very much less work: use
the left and right blank margins of the map for drawing the magnetic meridians.

You can still make use of the printed vertical division of the map, but this time construct the horizontal
side as a continuation of the line from cross to margin.
This is illustrated in the right-hand margin of the map
shown in Figure 9.1.

To use the magnetic meridians drawn by this method, slide the compass along your ruler to the margin of
the map, as described in Chapter 7, but align the lines
in the capsule with the line you have drawn rather
than with the printed margin of the map. In other
words you are aligning with a magnetic rather than a
geographic meridian.

Table 9.1 Offsets for drawing magnetic meridians (in millimeters; see Figure 9.1)

Declination (degrees)	7½' series, 1:24,000	15' series, 1:62,500	200-millimeter vertical, any scale
1	3	3	4
2	7	5	7
3	10	8	11
4	14	10	14
5	17	13	18
6	20	16	21
7	24	18	25
8	27	21	28
9	31	24	32
10	34	26	35
11	38	29	39
12	41	32	43
13	45	34	46
14	48	37	50
15	52	40	54
16	55	43	57
17	59	45	61
18	63	48	65
19	67	51	69
20	70	54	73
21	74	57	77
22	78	60	81
23	82	63	85
24	86	66	89
25	90	69	93
26	94	72	98
27	98	76	102
28	103	79	106
29	107	82	111
30	111	86	116
31	116	89	120
32	121	93	125
33	125	96	130
34	130	100	135
35	135	104	140

Correction by Arithmetic

The last method for adjusting for declination costs nothing and requires no drawing. But it takes some figure work and some rules.

Until now we have hardly ever read the degree scale of the compass. We have taken courses off the map and walked them, or taken bearings and plotted them on the map, without ever reading the numbers on the dial.

Those happy days are over. With this method you have to read the dial. Then you have to add or subtract the declination. Obviously it'll take different rules for declination East and declination West.

But that's not all. For each declination we'll need different rules for working from map to landscape (for example, taking a course off the map and then finding the compass setting to follow) and from landscape to map (for example, plotting a bearing).

That makes four rules in all.

Fortunately, you are not likely to jump back and forth from easterly declination to westerly. If you hike only in the Rockies you'll never have to bother about westerly declination; if you hike the Appalachian Trail you won't have to bother about easterly declination. (Don't worry about what happens when you cross the zero declination line—nothing happens. If you approach it from the West, the declination goes from an unimportant ½° East to nothing. And after you have hiked perhaps another 50 miles it becomes a still trivial ½° West.)

Unfortunately, the rules sound very much alike. So what I call the law of the key ring applies here.

When I have a half dozen keys I unfailingly get the right one. But with just two car keys I'm scratching my trunk trying to get the ignition key in place and trying to start the thing with the trunk key.

The rules resemble one another much more than the keys for your car, so the danger of getting the wrong one is greater. Also, if you pick the wrong car key nothing happens. When you use the wrong rule—by adding when you should be subtracting, or the other way around—you double the error of declination.

Using our map in 1982 as an example again, you'd be 24° off. For every mile you walk in what you think is the right direction, you go almost a half mile into the goony weeds.

One way to remember the rules is to write them, perhaps abbreviated and only the ones you need on a particular trip, on a card and glue it to your compass.

If you only operate in East declination—that is, in the western United States or western Canada—you need only two rules: one for map to field, and the other for field to map. Your card will read as follows:

> Map to field: subtract declination (E)
> Field to map: add declination (E)

Taking a course or the direction of some feature off the map for walking or locating the feature in the landscape is map to field: subtract.

Taking a bearing with the compass and plotting it on the map for identification or to get a position line is field to map: add.

There are a few tricks you should remember when you're doing the arithmetic. A circle consists of 360°. If after adding you get a figure larger than that, say 370°, subtract 360°; you'll get 10°.

If you have to subtract a declination larger than the dial reading, borrow 360° and add it to the dial reading. If the dial reads 10° and the declination to be subtracted is 12°, figure $10+360=370$; $370-12=358$. The answer is 358°.

In the first example you would have set the compass capsule until 10° was at the index mark; in the second, until it showed 358°.

When you get good at this sort of thing you can just turn the capsule the correct number of degrees in the right direction. Then you don't need the 360° gimmicks. By turning the dial clockwise (East) you subtract; by turning it the other way you add. You don't have to memorize that; you can see it on the compass scale.

The danger in the turn-the-dial method is that after starting you may forget where the dial was originally.

Here are examples for easterly declination 12°.

After you place your compass from start to destination and align the capsule with the map margin, the dial reads 180°. This is map to field, so you must subtract. You should get 168° either by arithmetic or by turning the capsule clockwise 12°. You now box the needle and walk in the direction indicated by the arrow.

After you take a bearing and box the needle, the dial of your compass reads 90°. This is field to map, so you must add. You should get 102° either by arithmetic or by turning the capsule counterclockwise 12°. You now align the lines in the capsule with the left or right margin of the map and are ready to plot the bearing on the map.

If you only operate in West declination—that is, in the eastern United States or eastern Canada—you again need only two rules: one for map to field, and one for field to map. Your card will read as follows:

> Map to field: add declination (W)
>
> Field to map: subtract declination (W)

Taking a course or the direction of some feature off the map for walking or locating the feature in the landscape is map to field: add.

Taking a bearing with the compass and plotting it on the map for identification or to get a position line is field to map: subtract.

Here are two examples for westerly declination 12°.

After you place your compass from start to destination and align the capsule with the vertical map margin, the dial reads 180°. That's map to field, so you must add. You should get 192° either by arithmetic or by turning the capsule counterclockwise 12°. You now box the needle and walk in the direction indicated by the arrow.

After you take a bearing and box the needle, the dial of your compass reads 90°. That's field to map, so you must subtract. You should get 78° either by arithmetic or by turning the capsule clockwise 12°.

Handling sums larger than 360° or subtracting declinations larger than the dial reading is of course the same as described above for easterly declination. Also, for both East and West declination, turning the dial clockwise, toward East, subtracts; turning the dial counterclockwise, toward West, adds.

I can imagine you being totally confused by all these rules. To help you reconstruct them I have made up a rhyme that's so silly you'll never forget it. Unfortunately, like so many memory aids, it needs some explanation. Here it is (it is also good advice when you sight a grizzly):

> Bear East,
> Turn West!

"Bear" stands for bearing, the most used field to map operation. "East" is short for declination East. "Turn" means the capsule of compass is to be turned.

The complete translation then is: handling bearings—field to map—in areas of East declination, turn the capsule toward W, counterclockwise.

All the other rules follow from this one. Handling map to field problems, such as walking a course, in areas of East declination must be the opposite from the handling of bearings. Turn the capsule toward E, clockwise.

Even where the declination is West, bears are to be avoided:

> Bear West,
> Turn East!

That is, bearings (and all field to map problems) in areas of West declination require turning the capsule toward E, clockwise.

Walking a course (and all map to field problems) in areas of West declination require the opposite treatment from bearings. You must turn the capsule toward the W, counterclockwise.

Logic of Corrections

Some readers may not care for silly bear tales and may worry about losing written instructions. They want something they can understand, and if necessary reconstruct.

I'll try to satisfy them. But it won't be easy, I warn you. And it's something that seems perfectly logical in your armchair, and totally escapes you when you are wet, hungry, blistered by sock and sun, and have lost the trail.

You have to recall that normally the numbers on the degree dial increase toward the right, clockwise, toward East. That's the basis of all that follows.

I'll use examples, starting again with declination East (such as in the western United States and Canada). That means the compass needle points to the East (right) of North.

Courses, Declination East. To walk a course toward true (geographic or map) North you must walk left, toward numbers lower than 360° on the compass. Hence, *subtract* the declination from courses taken from the map. Example: declination 15°E; you want to make a course of true North, 360°. That'll be 15° left of 360°; 345° is your compass course.

Bearings, Declination East. An object that gives a reading of 360° on your compass is to the right (toward higher numbers) of true North. Hence, *add* the declination to bearings to be transferred to the map. Example: declination 15°E; bearing by compass 360°. That is 15° to the right of true (map) North. You plot the bearing on the map as 15°.

If the declination is West (such as in the eastern United States and Canada), the compass needle points to the West (left) of North, and the rules are the other way around.

Courses, Declination West. To walk a course toward true (geographic or map) North you must walk right, toward numbers higher than 360° on the compass. *Add* the declination. Example: declination 15°W. You want to make a course of true North. That'll be 15° right of North (360 or 0°); 15° is your compass course.

Bearings, Declination West. An object that gives a reading of 360° on your compass is to the left (toward lower numbers) of true North. *Subtract* the declination. Example: declination 15°W; bearing by compass 360°. That is 15° to the left of true (map) North. You plot the bearing on the map as 345°.

There is a way to check yourself after you have performed any of these last four calculations. It makes use of an old saw (it was old when Captain Bligh was a midshipman) that goes like this:

> Declination East, compass least;
> Declination West, compass best.

That is true for the first two examples above (declination East); 345 is less than 360, and 0 is less than 15.

It is also true for the last two examples above (declination West); 15 is better than 0, and 360 is better than 345.

Remember that courses must be expressed in magnetic direction, while bearings are plotted on the map in true direction. Then you can check any calculation to see if it makes the compass reading least (for declination East) or best (for declination West).

Perhaps you'll convert to the method of lining maps, or at least drawing a few lines in the margins. Or you might even decide to get a compass with built-in adjustment for declination.

10.
Altimeter Navigation

A pocket altimeter, a device smaller than some base plate compasses and only a little heavier—about 3 ounces (90 grams)—can add another dimension to your navigation. It adds height.

Topographic maps, though themselves flat, indicate heights. With an instrument that measures heights we improve our ability to fix our position. At least in hilly or mountainous country. (When you are hiking in the Everglades in southern Florida, where the land slopes perhaps a dozen feet in 100 miles, knowing your height to the nearest 40 feet would not help your navigation.)

All altimeters are first cousins of barometers. Like barometers, they basically measure local air pressure. Since air pressure diminishes the higher you go, altimeter dials can be calibrated for reading off elevations in feet or meters.

Simple Uses for Altimeters

Even the least expensive altimeters, currently about $15, have their uses in mountain navigation. They let you estimate your progress.

If you know there's a 4000-foot climb ahead of you, an indication of 2000 feet above the valley tells you half the climb is behind you. If you had set the ring so the needle originally indicated zero, it would now indicate 2000 feet.

If the rest of the climb is not much steeper—the lines on the topo map are not closer together—and if the footway doesn't deteriorate, you can estimate your time of arrival. I'd figure a little more time for the next 2000 feet than for the first to allow for fatigue.

Some hikers schedule rest stops by elevation gained rather than by time. Say you plan on resting after every 1000 feet gained. It's a morale builder to let your party know you have already climbed 800 feet of the 1000. (Morale building is fine, but I rest when I get to water, shade, a boulder to rest my pack on, view points, rare flowers, or any other excuse rather than by altimeter or clock.)

On the way down rests are usually not so much in demand. But you can still keep track of your progress. Set the altimeter at the start to 4000 feet, for example. When the needle indicates 3000 you are a quarter down, at 2000 one-half, and so on.

This type of inexpensive altimeter is usually calibrated in 200-foot or 100-meter intervals, which lets you estimate your gain or loss of elevation to 100 feet or 50 meters.

That's certainly adequate for scheduling rest stops, roughly checking your progress, and estimating your time of arrival.

You can't expect much more for $15. But people do. And that's why many outdoor books either don't talk about altimeters at all, or warn that they are not much use "because they are influenced by the weather." They are, but that's not why the inexpensive altimeters will not help you in precision navigation.

The limitation lies in their simple construction. The heart of altimeters—and modern barometers—is a metal capsule that swells when the pressure drops and flattens when the pressure increases. The needle of the altimeter or barometer shows the movements of the capsule, much magnified.

Unfortunately the capsule also expands when it gets warmer and contracts when it gets chilled. And the needle magnifies these changes as well.

In some tests I did for an article in *Backpacker 24* I started several of these simple altimeters at 80°F (27°C), simulating the temperature in one's shirt pocket, then chilled them to 45° (7°C) at sea level. They indicated rises of 400 to 450 feet (130 meters), and took up to 30 minutes to indicate correctly when brought back to the original temperature.

In a second series of tests I chilled them to 20°F (−7°C). Some of the instruments indicated rises of up to 600 feet (180 meters), and took three-quarters of an hour to return to the correct reading at the original temperature.

There is a moral in all this: whatever altimeter you are using, don't warm it with your body and then expect it to show correct elevations when you take it out of your pocket. When you are hiking in shirtsleeves in cool weather, stuff a packet of moleskin between your chest and the altimeter. Carry your altimeter in a cool pocket rather than in your handwarmers. And don't set your altimeter, however sophisticated, in the warmth of a hut or cable car station and expect accurate performance.

When inexpensive altimeters are kept at constant temperature they are not too bad. In the heated cabin of a small plane the same instruments used in the tests above showed an error of 100 feet (30 meters) at 2000 feet (600 meters) above ground and an error of 300 feet (100 meters) at 5000 feet (1500 meters) above ground.

(In an airliner pocket altimeters indicate the cabin pressure, which is kept constant at some low level pressure. So your instrument may indicate 3000 feet (1000 meters) when the plane is flying at 30,000 feet (10 kilometers).)

Basic Altimeter Navigation

Better—and of course more expensive—altimeters compensate for the temperature of the instrument.

Theoretically that means the needle will not move when you warm or cool the instrument.

For such instruments it is worthwhile to check into the influence of moving weather systems on the altimeter reading. (With the inexpensive altimeters there is no use to worry about short-term, say hourly, weather influences.)

If you have watched barometers regularly, you'll seldom have seen movements of more than 1 inch, or 25 millimeters, of mercury (34 millibars) in 24 hours. That works out to 0.04 inches (1 millimeter) of mercury or about 1½ millibars per hour, which translates into about 40 feet (12 meters) elevation difference at 3000 feet (1000 meters) above sea level. (A little less lower down, somewhat more higher up.)

On most days the hourly change in barometric pressure, and with it the elevation error, will be a good

Figure 10.1 *Gischard altimeter. An economical, temperature-compensated instrument imported by Recreational Equipment, Inc., Seattle. Its highly legible scale is calibrated at 100-foot intervals.*

Figure 10.2 *Peet Bros. Model 88 altimeter, made in West Germany, is temperature compensated, reads altitudes to 18,000 feet in 6 turns of the needle, kept track of by the counter seen at the 6 o'clock position. Calibrated at 20-foot intervals. It weighs 3.5 oz., measures about 2½ × ¾ inches, and is said to be accurate to 40 feet over the entire range if used correctly.*

Figure 10.3 *Thommen Model TX altimeter, made in Switzerland, temperature compensated, comes in several ranges from 15,000 feet or 5,000 meters, to 27,000 feet or 9,000 meters. Model TX-18 shown here has a range of 21,000 feet, calibrated at 20-foot intervals. (Metric models are calibrated at 10-m intervals.) Weight and size as above. The TX series is said to be accurate to within 30 feet over the entire range if used correctly.*

deal less. But we should not neglect it with an instrument that's capable of giving accurate readings over a wide range of temperatures.

Surveyors long ago solved the problem neatly. They leave one instrument at the bottom of the mountain, while carrying another one to the elevation to be measured. Someone reads the instrument in the valley at short intervals and records the readings. When the surveyor returns he corrects his barometer readings according to the changes in the valley.

That method is not practical for hikers, skiers, and fishermen, but errors can be minimized.

All you do is this: At the trailhead, set the altimeter as accurately as possible to the elevation read there from the map. From here on the altimeter should show about the same elevation above sea level as your map does.

Then, whenever you come to a mapped point you can positively identify, reset the altimeter for the elevation given for that point. It could be at a side creek joining the creek you're following, a bridge, a saddle or peak, or a power line crossing your trail.

Once you start looking for them, you'll find such resetting points all the time.

But say you have walked off-trail for one hour without having been able to reset your elevation from the map.

As we have seen, it would be unusual for the weather to have fooled you by more than 40 feet (12 meters). In the mountains this is the usual contour interval on 7½' topo quads. On a mapped trail you'd know your position within one contour line. What more can you expect with so little effort in navigation?

Here's an example: you're climbing the La Poudre Pass trail, which takes off near the western border of section 7 on our map. You would have set your altimeter where the trail—at first a light-duty road—branches off from the medium-duty (red) road. There's a bench mark giving an elevation of 9095 feet just south of the branch-off, and the side road immediately crosses the 9080 contour, so you would have set your altimeter to 9080 feet.

Now your altimeter reads 9280 feet. Where are you?

You have two position lines. One is the La Poudre Pass trail. The other is the 9280 contour line. You must be at or near the point where the two position lines cross, not far from the Northeast corner of section 1.

Since you probably have been underway for less than an hour, the error from change in barometric pressure due to a weather system is not likely to be significant. I'd trust this position to, say, within one-half contour interval.

Another example: you are driving along the medium-duty road looking for the start of the Ute trail (in section 18).

"Have we passed it?"

Nobody in the car has counted curves, but you recall having checked the altimeter where you saw the La Poudre Pass trail branch off. It read, just as you had expected, about 9100 feet. It now reads 9900 feet.

One glance at the map and you can confidently announce, "No, we have some more climbing to do." You have not even reached the 10,000-foot contour, and the trail takes off between that and the 10,200-foot line.

By the way, the confidence in altimeter readings not changing much in one hour refers to observers moving slowly, on foot or perhaps by canoe or kayak. In an automobile you may approach a high or low pressure area fast enough to make hourly resettings of the altimeter too far apart.

As navigator on this road I'd certainly check and if necessary reset my altimeter at Milner Pass.

Here are a few more examples, illustrated by the contour map in Figure 10.4.

Example 1. You have set your altimeter at the confluence of two branches of a creek at point 1 near the road crossing. A bench mark there reads 3120 feet on the map. On the original map, which showed contours every 40 feet, you could also have found the elevation from the contour lines. (To keep matters simple, only the index contours at 200-foot intervals are shown).

Example 2. You have worked your way up the northern branch of the creek. Your altimeter now reads 3800 feet. You are at the crossing of two position lines, the mapped creek and the contour line; you must be at or near point 2.

Example 3. You are on the trail that enters near the southwestern corner of the map. Your altimeter now indicates 3600 feet. You must be at or near the intersection of two position lines, the trail and the 3600-foot elevation, point 3.

Example 4. You know how to fix your position from two compass bearings. They may be hard to come by

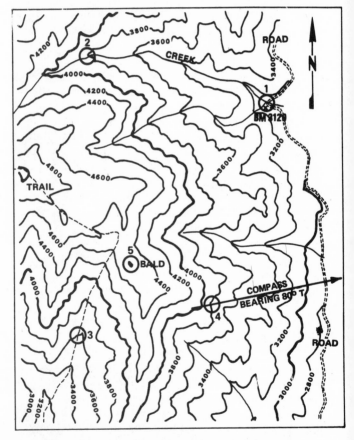

Figure 10.4 *Contour map for text examples of altimeter navigation.*

in a forest, where you'd be lucky to get an occasional glimpse of even one identifiable landmark. That'd be enough on a mapped trail, but here you have been bushwhacking. Now you get a glimpse of the fire tower on the next mountain. Corrected for declination, it bears 80°. Your altimeter now reads 3800 feet. You plot the bearing, your first position line, then look for the 3800-foot contour. You are where the two position lines—bearing and contour—cross, at or near point 4.

Note: you get the most reliable fix from a compass bearing at right angles to your trail. In the same way you get the best fix when the compass bearing crosses the contour line at about that angle.

You might think you could just as well be near point 3. But look closer; you would certainly know whether the higher ground was toward the West, as at point 4, or toward the North, as at point 3. You could not see the fire tower from point 3 because the mountain you're standing on is in the way.

Example 5. You are again on the trail used in example 3. You see the open area, locally known as a bald, near point 5. You climb it for the view. Glancing at the map, you notice it's the only isolated spot in the area that rises to 4600 feet. The sharp bend in the trail, which you can see from your lookout, makes you quite sure you've got the right point. Reset your altimeter here to 4600 feet.

So far all examples have dealt with using and resetting your altimeter while you were on the move.

Here's a trick for minimizing the effect of weather on your altimeter when you're not moving. When you arrive at your campsite, read your altimeter and write down the elevation. Stay a few hours, a night, or a week. When you are ready to leave, set the altimeter to the elevation recorded at your arrival. That'll be far more accurate than the actual reading, which may be off by a few hundred feet after just one night.

Some people find it hilarious that their sleeping bags have risen, or fallen, a couple of hundred feet while they slept. But I'd be worried if my altimeter didn't show some change. I'd suspect rigor mortis.

Effects of Nonstandard Air Temperatures

When you come to try your altimeter, you'll find that your navigation doesn't turn out quite as neatly as my examples. You'll begin to see why I wrote "at or near" over and over.

If you use an altimeter that's said to be temperature compensated (such as a Gischard or a Thommen 1000) and easily read to the nearest 30 feet (10 meters), you'll find at each resetting point that your instrument is somewhat off. Even in settled weather, when experience tells you that the barometric pressure can't have changed significantly in the hour since you last reset the altimeter, it will not quite agree with the elevation on the map.

That's not the fault of the altimeter. It'd be a coincidence if the altimeter did read exactly right.

I'm not talking about inadequate temperature compensation. (Both instruments performed well on my chill tests.) There is a fundamental reason for even the very best altimeters to seem somewhat off. It has to do with the atmosphere itself.

Altimeters are designed, built, and tested according to a theoretical atmosphere in which the air pressure diminishes in a certain way while at the same time the temperature drops steadily as you go higher up.

The sea-level temperature in that atmosphere is assumed to be 15°C (59°F) and to drop steadily by 6.5°C per 1000 meters (about 3.6°F per 1000 feet) in the altitudes that interest us. It is most unlikely that on any given day the air temperature where you are is exactly what the standard calibration of altimeters assumes it to be.

A perfectly temperature-compensated altimeter ignores the local temperature. But the column of air that weighs down on the barometric cell in your instrument does not. It is denser (heavier) when it's colder, and thinner (lighter) when it's warmer, than the simple formula assumes.

If the air through which you climbed averaged 20°F warmer than the standard atmosphere shows, the altimeter will indicate about 960 feet gained when it should indicate 1000 feet.

If the air through which you climbed averaged 20°F cooler than the standard atmosphere shows, the altimeter will indicate a gain of about 1040 feet.

Metric examples: if the air was 10°C warmer than the standard atmosphere assumes, the altimeter will indicate a gain of 965 meters when it should show a gain of 1000 meters. If the air was 10°C cooler than the standard atmosphere assumes, it will indicate a gain of about 1035 meters.

When you are going down, the altimeter will act in the same erroneous manner as it did on the way up. That has to be so; if you ran up and down the same vertical distance, the altimeter should show the same reading at the end of your trip as at the start.

> When the air is *warmer* than standard, the altimeter
> *underestimates* the *change* in elevation (up or down).

> When the air is *cooler* than standard, the altimeter
> *overestimates* the *change* in elevation (up or down).

The error encountered when you are climbing is quite straightforward. But when you are going down it is a bit tricky. Assume in the first example (air warmer than standard) that you were starting out downhill from 1000 feet. At sea level, having been carried down 1000 feet, your altimeter will only show a 960 foot drop and indicate an elevation of 40 feet above sea level.

It's shy 40 feet going up or going down. But the elevation indicated is too low going up, too high going down.

Table 10.1 will help give you a feel for whether local temperature is warmer or cooler than the corresponding standard atmosphere temperature.

The best way to get acquainted with your altimeter, short of using it on actual hikes, is to take it for an automobile ride through the mountains while someone else drives. That also gives you more reference points in one hour than you'd find on the trail in a day or more.

Take an air thermometer along. If everyone in the car can stand it, use neither heater nor air conditioner. Leave a window open and don't let the sun shine on your altimeter and thermometer.

Then watch for places along the road where the elevation is posted. Mountain passes and overlooks are good resetting points. In many states the elevation appears on the signs that mark town limits. This is probably not the elevation of the sign but of the post office or city hall. I'd disregard such signs in towns built on a slope.

When you find a trustworthy posted elevation write it down along with the reading of your altimeter.

Here is the discrepancy you can expect for nonstandard temperatures:

> For every degree Fahrenheit expect a 2-foot error for every 1000-foot change in elevation.

> For every degree Celsius expect a 4-meter error for every 1000-meter change in elevation.

Table 10.1 Standard atmosphere, temperatures used in calibrating altimeters

English units		Metric units	
Elevation (feet)	*Temperature (°F)*	*Elevation (meters)*	*Temperature (°C)*
Sea level	59	Sea level	15
2000	52	500	12
4000	45	1000	8½
6000	38	1500	5
8000	31	2000	+2
10,000	23	2500	−1½
12,000	16	3000	−4½
14,000	9	3500	−8
16,000	2	4000	−11

On one particular ride you are not likely to encounter temperatures both above and below the standard temperatures for the given elevations. (It is possible though.) In summer you are likely to get only warmer temperatures, in winter only cooler ones. So you won't get complete examples of effects of atmospheric temperature on your readings. But you will be going up and down and see for yourself how variations in temperature affect altimeter readings.

In warmer than standard air the elevations indicated are lower than posted after a climb, and higher than posted after a descent.

In cooler than standard air the elevations will be higher than posted after a climb and lower than posted after a descent.

These statements assume, of course, that you reset your altimeter to the elevation at the start of the climb or descent.

If you plan to hike in the European Alps, you can get acquainted with your altimeter on the train. Railroad stations there prominently display their elevation above sea level.

Precision Altimeter Navigation

If you plan to use the Gischard or Thommen 1000 altimeters, you've probably already found out more than you want to know about altimetry. Much of the time the errors due to nonstandard temperature are not going to be larger than instrument errors due to incomplete temperature compensation combined with inaccuracy in setting and reading the instrument.

But with an altimeter such as the Thommen 2000 it pays to correct for nonstandard temperatures. That altimeter, according to its manufacturer, leaves the factory accurate within 30 feet (10 meters) anywhere from sea level to 15,000 feet (5000 meters) at temperatures of from $-4°F$ to $+86°F$ ($-20°C$ to $+30°C$).

I know of shortcuts in the calculation of the temperature correction, and have seen diagrams for calculating it, but none of them seems simple enough to me. So I have designed an alignment chart that makes finding the temperature correction as simple as I can make it.

Actually I designed two charts, one for English units and one for metric units. The most difficult part in using these two charts is using the right one; the rest is rather simple.

Obviously, you have to carry a thermometer to make the correction; you can get one that weighs less than one ounce (30 grams). When you set your altimeter or reset it at intermediate points, write down the elevation, perhaps in the margin of your topo map. Read the air temperature and write that down too.

Air temperature must be taken in the shade.
A good way to get the air temperature quickly is to whirl the thermometer on its lanyard for perhaps one minute. If that's too much bother, hang it from a branch for a few minutes. Don't lay it on cool moss or a hot rock.

When you come to read the altimeter, take the temperature again.

Now comes the hard part. If you use feet and degrees Fahrenheit, go to the chart titled English Units (Figure 10.5); if you use meters and degrees Celsius, go to the chart titled Metric Units (Figure 10.7).

On the left scale, labeled Mean Height, of the correct chart, mark the elevation at the point where you last set the altimeter (which I'll call *set point*) and also where you are now reading the altimeter (which I'll call *read point*). Estimate by eye the midpoint between the two marks, and mark that too.

Next mark the temperatures at the set point and the read point on the middle scale, labeled Mean Temperature. Again estimate the midpoint and mark it.

Now comes the final operation. Lay a straightedge on the chart—the thermometer, its case, or your ruler—through the midpoints on the two scales and read the figure and its sign on the right-hand scale, labeled Corr'n. This correction is for every 1000 feet (or meters) change in elevation. Its sign is for ascending.

You must now do a calculation. Adjust the correction for 1000 units (feet or meters) for the number of units you have actually covered. If you have covered

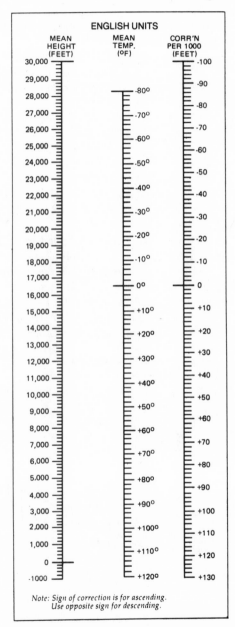

Figure 10.5 *Temperature correction chart for altimeters (English units).*

500 vertical feet (or meters), for example, you halve the correction found in the diagram.

If the sign of the correction is plus, you add; if it's minus, you subtract. If you have been going down to reach your present position, switch signs—add for minus and subtract for plus.

Example: At the set point the elevation was 4000 feet, the air temperature 70°F. Make a mark at 4000 on the left (height) scale; make another at 70 on the middle (temperature) scale.

At the read point the elevation is 6000 feet on your altimeter, the air temperature 64°F. Make a mark at 6000 on the left scale, and another at 64 on the middle scale.

Next mark the halfway points (circled in Figure 10.6). Draw a line through these points, or just lay your straightedge across them. At the point where the line (or straightedge) crosses the right (correction) scale, read the correction: +58 feet per 1000 feet climbed.

Since you climbed twice that height (from 4000 to 6000 feet), you double the correction ($2\times58=116$); since it is marked plus, you add the correction. Your present elevation is about 6120 feet.

Had you started at 6000 feet and 64°F and gone down to 4000 feet and 70°F, you would get the same

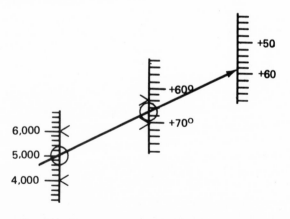

Figure 10.6 *Use of temperature correction chart shown in Figure 10.5.*

numerical result. But for going down you reverse the sign. The correction becomes −116 feet, and the corrected present elevation is about 3880 feet.

Metric example: At the set point the elevation was 1700 meters, the air temperature 17°C. Make a mark at 1700 meters on the left (height) scale; make another mark at +17 on the middle (temperature) scale.

At the read point the elevation shown on your altimeter is 2300 meters, the air temperature is 13°C. Make a mark at 2300 on the left (height) scale; make another mark at +13 on the middle (temperature) scale.

Next mark the halfway points (circled in Figure 10.8). Draw a line through these points, or just lay your straightedge across them. At the point where the line (or straightedge) crosses the right (correction) scale, read the correction: very close to +50 meters per 1000 meters climbed.

Since you climbed only six-tenths of that distance (from 1700 to 2300 meters), you multiply the correction by six-tenths ($6/10 \times 50 = 30$); since it is marked plus, you add 30 meters. Your present elevation is about 2330 meters.

Had you set your altimeter at 2330 meters and 13°C and walked down to the original set point, your altimeter now would read 1730 meters. If the temperature there was still 17°C you'd get virtually the same numerical result for the correction. But for going down you reverse the sign. The correction becomes −30 meters, the corrected present elevation about 1700 meters as before.

Mathematically inclined readers may think my method for getting *mean* height and *mean* temperature a bit simple. They'd add the elevation at the set point and the read point and divide the sum by two to get the mean elevation.

They'd also add the air temperatures at the set point and the read point and divide that sum by two to get the mean temperature.

The resulting corrections will be the same, of course.

If you work on metric maps—maps that give elevations in meters—you'll need a thermometer with a Cel-

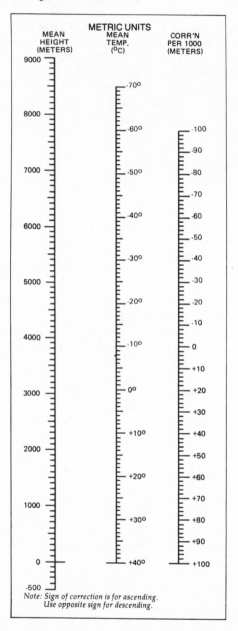

Figure 10.7 *Temperature correction chart for altimeters (metric units).*

sius scale, or perhaps both Fahrenheit and Celsius scales, to use the correction charts.

If you don't go in for maximum accuracy, perhaps because of limitations in your instrument, you can get along with an altimeter calibrated in feet, even when your map gives elevations in meters.

I proved that on a recent trip; where I had a piece of paper glued to my altimeter that read:

> 100 meters = 328 feet
> 1000 feet = 305 meters

I got in some extra minutes of rest whenever I calculated the conversions on the margin of my map.

Altimeters and the Weather

Many altimeters, even very inexpensive ones, have scales that show barometric pressure. Four different scales are in common use: inches of mercury, millimeters of mercury (also called Torrs after Torricelli, the inventor of the mercury barometer), millibars, and Pascals, which differ from millibars only in the placement of the decimal point.

The units of the scales matter little. Barometers are rotten predictors of weather. You may have heard or read differently, but predicting weather from your ba-

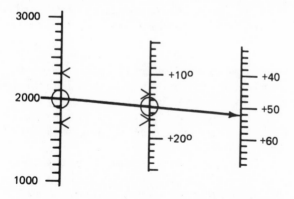

Figure 10.8 *Use of temperature correction chart shown in Figure 10.7.*

rometer puts you about where weather forecasting was around 1840, before distant observations were transmitted by telegraph.

Such predictions are usually based on "high glass" or "low glass." Unfortunately, except at or near sea level, you can't tell from your altimeter/barometer whether the glass is higher or lower than standard.

But isn't the barometer reading reduced to sea level when the altimeter is set to your present elevation?

Contrary to what your instruction booklet may lead you to believe, it is not.

To reduce barometric readings at stations far from sea level, the minimum and maximum temperatures during the last 12 hours, the humidity, and a few other factors have to be fed into an awkward formula. "Far" here may mean less than 3000 feet (1000 meters) when the atmosphere is a few degrees warmer or colder than the standard atmosphere. The more the temperature differs from the standard atmosphere and the higher the elevation, the harder it becomes to judge whether the pressure is actually high or low.

Many people claim good results in forecasting the weather not from the actual barometer reading but from its tendency—whether it is steady, falling, or rising, and how quickly it is changing if it is changing at all. Unfortunately, there is no simple way to decide what the barometer is doing when you're on the move.

These facts should discourage anyone from predicting the weather from nothing but the barometric pressure or its change—or from these factors combined with the wind direction.

Even the wind direction in the mountains is not necessarily the true wind direction. A valley that tends North-South will have northerly or southerly winds, but don't look for East and West winds other than purely local breezes caused by warming or cooling of the slopes.

If you're wrong in your forecast in the city, it usually doesn't matter much. But it's different in the mountains, where overconfident forecasts can lead you to a stream that has become impassable because of an unexpected downpour; or up a mountain for a view that is obliterated by clouds by the time you get there; or along a trail that disappears entirely because of a freak snowstorm, possibly endangering your life.

Moral: use your altimeter only for measuring elevations. With frequent resettings, a good instrument will serve you well.

The more frequent the better. The makers of the Thommen altimeters recommend keeping vertical distance between resettings to 500 meters (1600 feet), and the horizontal distance to 10 kilometers (6 miles).

Don't forget that regardless of how much you paid for your temperature-compensated altimeter, it needs correcting for nonstandard atmospheric temperature. Conditions, of course, are hardly ever anywhere near standard. After a few tries you'll develop a feel for when you should correct for greatest accuracy.

If you carry your altimeter along well-trodden or well-marked trails, you'll use it mostly to confirm your position, which is never much in doubt anyway.

I have done just that during the last five summers in Colorado, Wyoming, Montana, Idaho, and the Austrian Alps. And not just to prove to myself what a smart little navigator I was. I worked out altimeter problems as I went along so I'd remember how to do it under stress some day when I might really need to.

Sooner or later a well-marked trail peters out, or we decide to bushwhack. I'm not even talking about being temporarily uncertain of my position (the less polite phrase for that is being hopelessly lost). Then you want all the accuracy you can get.

Altimeter and Slope

Recently I read about an interesting application of an altimeter for position finding in poor visibility. It was originally described by Dr. Leopold Vietoris of Innsbruck in *Der Bergsteiger*. His method could be translated as navigation by the lay of the land.

The idea is simple. When you know approximately where on the map you are, you can sometimes pinpoint your position from the contour line (indicated by your altimeter) and the direction of the slope (from your compass), two position lines.

Figure 10.9 illustrates the idea. The slope is the direction in which water would run down. On the map it is the shortest connection from your contour line to the one below (see top left corner of the sketch).

In the landscape, even in fog, you can simulate your contour line by looking a bit forward or backward and trying to keep some target at the level of your eyes. Then imagine a line drawn between the target and you. Next get the direction at right angles to that line, heading down; that's the slope line.

A companion on skis, snowshoes, or on foot can make it easier to find the contour in the landscape. Have him or her take a position on your level but 30 to 100 feet (10 to 30 meters), depending on visibility,

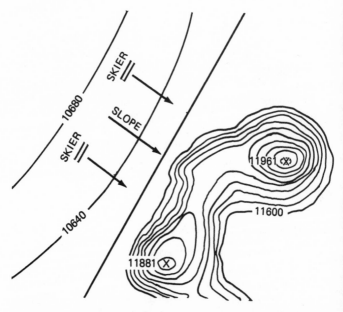

Figure 10.9 *Navigation by altimeter and the lay of the land. Left: two skiers determine the slope. Right: terrain where the method would be useful.*

away from you. The slope tends in the direction of a right angle to the line between you.

If you both have compasses you might take independent estimates of the slope direction as a check.

Now look at the twin peaks illustrated in the bottom right of Figure 10.9.

If your altimeter places you on the 11,600 contour and the slope drops off to the North, you must be about North of the 11,961 peak on that line. If the slope tends 270° (West), you are West and a bit South of the peak labeled 11,881. Or you could be West of the 11,961 peak. Another estimate of the slope after a short walk along the contour will let you decide which was the correct position. That method would work nearly everywhere in the vicinity of these peaks.

I have not had an opportunity to try the method in the field. Fog, mountains, and especially snow are not readily available where I live in southern Florida.

So I tried it on various areas of several topo maps. You can see that it would not pinpoint your position on our map West of the Colorado in sections 1, 12, and 13, where the contours are almost straight, but it's a technique to keep in mind.

11.
Direction from the Sky: North of the Tropics

I t is not often that a party finds itself without a compass. And compasses aren't likely to give up on you suddenly. Granted, you can lose a compass if it's not tied to you with a lanyard. Or you may have left it behind at last night's campsite. But it's not likely that all members of a party will lose their compasses, or leave them somewhere and not notice until hours away.

Unless you travel in a party of one.

You have been told not to by many experts. But some of us travel solo by necessity; none of our buddies can get away at the right time. Others solo by choice, balancing the rewards against the risks.

I can't repeat the customary warning, having ski-toured for years by myself. But I was lucky. I managed, for instance, to sprain my ankles where I could get to a doctor under my own power.

The soloist should always carry a spare compass.

So why bother with finding directions from the sky?

No book on land navigation would be complete without this information. Also, certain endlessly repeated methods for finding your way without a compass simply don't work, or work very poorly. I feel I owe you a warning about those.

And perhaps the best reason of all, navigation by sun and stars can add to your fun. At the very least it could be compared to learning about edible wild plants. After a nibble or two you can decide to stick to your freeze-dried diet.

So let's assume you find yourself without a compass. Where can you get directions?

Forget about the moss on the north side of trees. In some places it grows on all sides of the trunk, in others on none. That's been already pointed out by other authors.

Trees may or may not betray the direction of the prevailing winds by their lean or growth. Not very good.

Eventually everybody comes up with the sun and the stars.

To keep matters simple I'll restrict the discussion in this chapter to the Northern Hemisphere north of the tropics. The next chapter covers the tropics and the Southern Hemisphere.

Popular But Inaccurate Methods

Finding South from the Sun and a Watch

The instructions for this method are deceptively simple. First, point the hour hand toward the sun. Some authors may suggest using a match or something similar to cast a shadow for aligning the hour hand with the sun. South is then halfway between the hour hand and twelve o'clock on your dial.

The logic behind this method sounds convincing. The earth turns on its axis—which makes the sun seem to travel through the sky—once in 24 hours. The sun is south at noon. And the hour hand turns once around in 12 hours. That's where the halfway instruction comes from.

The method works nicely near the North Pole in summer. It works fairly well in Alaska, northern Canada, and other lands in the same latitudes.

In the northernmost parts of the contiguous United States it indicates within 7° from the true direction during the six winter months. In midsummer it's off as much as 23° either East or West of true South.

As you move southward, the error increases—to 24° in Key West (latitude 25°N) in the winter months, and to more than 70° in summer.

What was wrong with the logic? Nothing, except that it did not take into account that the sun in summer is high in the sky, whereas you hold your watch horizontally. Put differently, the sun's apparent movement does complete the 24th part of a full 360° circle around the earth in each hour, or 15° per hour. But the sun's bearing, measured on the horizon with a compass, is far from that. For example, in midsummer in Key West the sun changes a mere 5° between 6 and 7 A.M. (all times local mean time). Between 11 A.M. and noon it changes bearing 86°.

You may think Key West is just too far south for this method. But halfway between the southern and northern limits of the contiguous United States, at latitude 37°N, the summer error still reaches an intolerable 32°.

You'd have to go to the Brooks Range of Alaska, north of the Arctic Circle, to get the error down to about 10° in summer. In winter the maximum error there is down to 3°.

All these figures assume that you align the hour hand exactly with the sun, say by the shadow method. They also assume that you have allowed for daylight saving time by subtracting one hour when it's in effect. They further assume that you have corrected for the difference in longitude between your position and your standard time meridian, and that you have made yet another correction—for the time of noon itself—about which you'll read presently. These last corrections can easily amount to another three-quarters of an hour.

All these corrections get accurate results within 7° between latitudes 37°N and 49°N during the cool six months! (See Table 11.3)

If you ever have to fall back on the sun-and-watch method, you can narrow down the error as follows:

> In the morning, when the sun is East of South, the error is also East of South.
>
> In the afternoon, when the sun is West of South, the error is also West of South.

Finding East from the Motion of a Stick's Shadow

Another method you may have heard or read about makes use of the shadow the tip of a vertical object casts on the ground.

The logic sounds unimpeachable: since the sun seems to move from East to West, the shadow must move from West to East.

Plant a stick, say four feet long—or a ski pole, tip up in the snow—and mark the point where the tip's shadow falls now; wait about 15 minutes and again mark the point where the shadow falls.

A line connecting these points will run West-East, the second point being the more easterly.

The method sounds appealing. It requires no watch. You could smoke a pipe, or do a hundred push-ups, or just rest until the shadow has moved far enough to tell in what direction it's moving.

Since time is not involved, you don't have to use any of the corrections that the watch method entails. And East and West, of course, are just as good direction as North or South for finding all other directions.

I can see difficulties at some locations finding a soft spot in which to errect your 4-foot shadow pole. The vertical is no great problem; you could improvise a plumb line from a fishing line, dental floss, or whatever. The real problem is the area on which the shadow is to fall. It must be level and horizontal.

But even when it's used on level ground, this method is not as logical as it sounds. While moving westward, the sun also rises (before noon) or drops (after noon). The method seems to imply that this movement doesn't amount to much in 15 minutes.

Table 11.1 Bearing of sunrise (in degrees)

Date	Latitude, North or South							
	25°	34°	40°	44°	47°	50°	52°	54°
Jan. 1	116	118	121	123	125	127	129	132
16	113	116	118	120	122	124	126	128
25	111	113	115	117	119	120	122	124
Feb. 2	109	111	112	114	115	117	118	120
8	107	108	110	111	112	114	115	116
15	104	106	107	108	109	110	111	113
20	102	103	104	105	106	107	108	109
26	100	101	102	103	103	104	105	105
Mar. 3	98	98	99	100	100	101	101	102
8	96	96	97	97	97	98	98	99
13	93	94	94	94	94	95	95	95
18	91	91	91	91	91	92	92	92
23	89	89	89	89	89	88	88	88
29	87	86	86	86	86	85	85	85
Apr. 3	84	84	83	83	83	82	82	81
8	82	82	81	80	80	79	79	78
13	80	79	78	77	77	76	75	75
19	78	77	76	75	74	73	72	71
25	76	74	73	72	71	70	69	67
May 1	73	72	70	69	68	66	65	64
8	71	69	68	66	65	63	62	60
16	69	67	65	63	61	60	58	56
26	67	64	62	60	58	56	54	52
June 10	64	62	59	57	55	53	51	48
30	64	62	59	57	55	53	51	48

I simulated the movement of the shadow on a computer. The deviation from true East depends on your latitude, the date, and the time of day. I'll spare you the details, because nowhere in the latitude of the contiguous United States can you get consistent results with errors of less than 20° or 30°.

Planting the pole so that at first it does not cast a shadow at all—that is, facing the sun—does not improve the result. The moon's shadow is equally unsatisfactory, at times more so.

Table 11.1 continued

Date	Latitude, North or South							
	25°	34°	40°	44°	47°	50°	52°	54°
July 1	64	62	59	57	55	53	51	48
19	67	64	62	60	58	56	54	52
28	69	67	65	63	61	60	58	56
Aug. 5	71	69	68	66	65	63	62	60
12	73	72	70	69	68	66	65	64
19	76	74	73	72	71	70	69	67
25	78	77	76	75	74	73	72	71
30	80	79	78	77	77	76	75	75
Sept. 5	82	82	81	80	80	79	79	78
10	84	84	83	83	83	82	82	81
16	87	86	86	86	86	85	85	85
21	89	89	89	89	89	88	88	88
26	91	91	91	91	91	92	92	92
Oct. 1	93	94	94	94	94	95	95	95
6	96	96	97	97	97	98	98	99
11	98	98	99	100	100	101	101	102
17	100	101	102	103	103	104	105	105
22	102	103	104	105	106	107	108	109
28	104	106	107	108	109	110	111	113
Nov. 3	107	108	110	111	112	114	115	116
10	109	111	112	114	115	117	118	120
18	111	113	115	117	119	120	122	124
27	113	116	118	120	122	124	126	128
Dec. 11	116	118	121	123	125	127	129	132
31	116	118	121	123	125	127	129	132

Recommended Methods

The Bearing of the Sun at Sunrise and Sunset

This method requires no equipment whatever, just the sun. It is the method by which ships at sea have checked their compasses and determined compass error, and variation (called declination ashore), for the last two centuries.

With the Nautical Almanac of the year and a knowledge of his latitude, the navigator calculates the

Table 11.2 Bearing of sunset (in degrees)

Date	Latitude, North or South							
	25°	34°	40°	44°	47°	50°	52°	54°
Jan. 1	244	242	239	237	235	233	231	228
16	247	244	242	240	238	236	234	232
25	249	247	245	243	241	240	238	236
Feb. 1	251	249	248	246	245	243	242	240
8	253	252	250	249	248	246	245	244
14	256	254	253	252	251	250	249	247
20	258	257	256	255	254	253	252	251
25	260	259	258	257	257	256	255	255
Mar. 3	262	262	261	260	260	259	259	258
8	264	264	263	263	263	262	262	261
13	267	266	266	266	266	265	265	265
18	269	269	269	269	269	268	268	268
23	271	271	271	271	271	272	272	272
29	273	274	274	274	274	275	275	275
Apr. 3	276	276	277	277	277	278	278	279
8	278	278	279	280	280	281	281	282
13	280	281	282	283	283	284	285	285
19	282	283	284	285	286	287	288	289
25	284	286	287	288	289	290	291	293
May 1	287	288	290	291	292	294	295	296
8	289	291	292	294	295	297	298	300
16	291	293	295	297	299	300	302	304
26	293	296	298	300	302	304	306	308
June 10	296	298	301	303	305	307	309	312
30	296	298	301	303	305	307	309	312

bearing of the sun at sunrise or sunset, accurate to a tenth of one degree.

We don't need such accurate results and would like to eliminate calculations as much as possible. We would also like results that don't need a new table every year.

Tables 11.1 and 11.2 provide the necessary information for any year, including leap years, at least until the year 2000. They cover latitudes from the tropics to 54°N. Beyond that latitude the method becomes too inaccurate due to the small angle between the sun's apparent orbit and the horizon.

Table 11.2 continued

Date	Latitude, North or South							
	25°	34°	40°	44°	47°	50°	52°	54°
July 1	296	298	301	303	305	307	309	312
19	293	296	298	300	302	304	306	308
28	291	293	295	297	299	300	302	304
Aug. 5	289	291	292	294	295	297	298	300
12	287	288	290	291	292	294	295	296
18	284	286	287	288	289	290	291	293
24	282	283	284	285	286	287	288	289
30	280	281	282	283	283	284	285	285
Sept. 4	278	278	279	280	280	281	281	282
10	276	276	277	277	277	278	278	279
15	273	274	274	274	274	275	275	275
20	271	271	271	271	271	272	272	272
26	269	269	269	269	269	268	268	268
Oct. 1	267	266	266	266	266	265	265	265
6	264	264	263	263	263	262	262	261
11	262	262	261	260	260	259	259	258
16	260	259	258	257	257	256	255	255
22	258	257	256	255	254	253	252	251
28	256	254	253	252	251	250	249	247
Nov. 3	253	252	250	249	248	246	245	244
9	251	249	248	246	245	243	242	240
17	249	247	245	243	241	240	238	236
26	247	244	242	240	238	236	234	232
Dec. 11	244	242	239	237	235	233	231	228
31	244	242	239	237	235	233	231	228

The precision of maritime tables is not warranted on land. Unlike the horizon at sea, on land the horizon almost everywhere is not a nice sharp horizontal line.

The bearing of the rising or setting sun is calculated for the time when—at sea—the sun is about one-half of its diameter above the horizon.

It doesn't matter much how high you are when your horizon is at about the same level. Don't fret when you miss the actual sunrise or sunset by minutes, or when it takes place behind some low obstruction. Right after rising and just before setting the sun changes bearing rather slowly. For example, to change its bearing by a single degree takes it nine minutes at Key West (latitude 25°N), seven minutes in the middle of the contiguous United States (latitude 35°N), and five minutes at the limit of the table (latitude 54°N).

With a reasonably unobstructed horizon, it is unlikely that all the errors related to year, date, elevation, and your estimate of the actual horizon will result in a bearing that is off by more than two degrees.

That may not be good enough to set the declination on your compass when better information is available to you. But it's certainly good enough to estimate North or any other direction when you find yourself without a compass.

Table 11.1 is for sunrise, with easterly bearings (48° to 132°), and Table 11.2 is for sunset, with westerly bearings (228° to 312°). For approximate bearings of sunrise or sunset, say for orienting your map or for siting your tent to catch the first rays of the sun, simply use the nearest date and the latitude nearest you. Read the bearing of sunrise or sunset where the line of the date crosses the column of latitude.

Example: Sunrise on August 9 at latitude 41°30'N. Using nearest date (August 12) and nearest latitude (40°N) you'd get a bearing of 70°. For sunset on the same day and at the same latitude you'd get 290°.

If you need greater accuracy you can interpolate. August 9 is about halfway between August 5 and 12. So the middle value for latitude 40°N—between 68° and 70°, or 69°—would be a closer value. The latitude is about halfway between 40°N and 44°N, so again the mid-value would be closer. Taking off one degree should allow for that: 68° is about as close as you could come.

If you glance at the lines and columns in the tables you'll find that 2° and 3° are the most common intervals between neighboring entries. So the interpolated result is usually very close to the figure you get simply by taking the nearest date and nearest latitude.

Here's an example from the sunset table: July 22, latitude 45°45'N. The nearest date (July 19) and latitude (47°) gives 302 for the sunset bearing. You could interpolate as follows: between July 19 and the next date,

July 28, are nine days, in which the bearing diminishes 3°. July 22 is one-third into that period, so subtracting 1° seems indicated. The latitude is almost halfway between 47°N and 44°N, where the bearing is 2° less. So another degree subtracted would make the best estimate 300°.

You don't have to carry this book with you to have all the data you need for a given trip. Unless you hike the entire 2000 miles or so of the Appalachian Trail and spend half a year doing it, the data you need will fit on part of a small file card. A few lines of dates and at most two columns of latitude will do for most trips.

Finding South from the Bearing of the Sun at Noon

A slightly more accurate method for getting a bearing from the sun requires correct time—correct to the nearest half minute. A few years ago that would have stopped almost anyone from reading on. Few people took watches skiing, fishing, or hiking that would be so accurate a week from the trailhead. But now even affordable watches keep time that close, and closer.

The principle of getting direction from the sun at noon is simple: in the area covered by this chapter the sun at local noon bears exactly South, by definition.

The practical problem is to find the exact time of local apparent noon. Nothing else will do. The change of bearing of the sun is greatest at noon; that's why we have to be so accurate.

If the earth's orbit were a circle, and if the earth's axis were at right angles to the orbit, the sun would bear South every day at 12:00 noon local mean time (*mean* refers to the time that all clocks keep, based on a day that is exactly 24 hours long). The actual orbit is an ellipse, and the earth's axis is inclined about 23½° from the vertical. These two facts combine to make the sun bear South anywhere from one-quarter hour before to one-quarter hour after noon, local mean time.

The real sun's time of bearing south, local apparent noon (sundial noon), is shown in Table 11.3 for every day of any year in terms of local mean time.

If your watch showed local mean time on August 5

Table 11.3 Local mean time of noon

Date	Noon	Date	Noon
Jan. 1–2	12:03	Apr. 1	12:04
3–4	12:04	2–5	12:03
5–6	12:05	6–7	12:02
7–9	12:06	8–12	12:01
10–12	12:07	13–17	12:00
13	12:08	18–19	11:59
14–16	12:09	20–26	11:58
17–20	12:10	27–30	11:57
21–22	12:11	May 1–5	11:57
23–28	12:12	6–24	11:56
29–31	12:13	25–31	11:57
Feb. 1–6	12:13	June 1–2	11:57
7–17	12:14	3–9	11:58
18–27	12:13	10–12	11:59
28–29	12:12	13–18	12:00
Mar. 1–5	12:12	19–23	12:01
6–7	12:11	24–26	12:02
8–12	12:10	27–30	12:03
13–16	12:09	July 1–2	12:03
17–18	12:08	3–9	12:04
19–22	12:07	10–14	12:05
23–26	12:06	15–31	12:06
27–28	12:05	Aug. 1–7	12:06
29–31	12:04	8–12	12:05

you'd expect the sun to bear South at 12:06 P.M. But nobody's watch is set to local time, except by accident.

There are good practical reasons for setting our watches to some form of standard time. When it's 12:00 noon local mean time in Washington D.C., it's 12:40 P.M. in Eastport, Maine, and 11:44 A.M. in Savannah, Georgia. At one time each of these cities actually operated on its own time. As a result U.S. railroad timetables used at least 56 different times. That's no way to run railroads! So since November 18, 1883, the United States has been on the four standard times we are still using.

Eastern Standard Time is the local mean time of any place at longitude 75°W. When it's local mean noon

Table 11.3 continued

Date	Noon	Date	Noon
13–18	12:04	26–31	11:43
19–23	12:03	Nov. 1–12	11:43
24–25	12:02	13–16	11:44
26–29	12:01	17–21	11:45
30–31	12:00	22–26	11:46
Sept. 1–2	12:00	27	11:47
3–4	11:59	28–30	11:48
5–8	11:58	Dec. 1	11:48
9–11	11:57	2–4	11:49
12–13	11:56	5	11:50
14–16	11:55	6–8	11:51
17–20	11:54	9–11	11:52
21	11:53	12	11:53
22–25	11:52	13–15	11:54
26–28	11:51	16–17	11:55
29–30	11:50	18	11:56
Oct. 1–4	11:49	19–21	11:57
5–8	11:48	22–23	11:58
9–10	11:47	24	11:59
11–15	11:46	25–27	12:00
16–21	11:45	28–29	12:01
22–25	11:44	30–31	12:02

there it's also noon in Washington, D.C., Eastport, and Savannah.

Theoretically the Eastern Standard Time zone extends 7½° of longitude East and West of the standard meridian, 75°W. That should leave out Eastport (67°W), which is just outside the eastern limit of that zone. But many small adjustments such as this have been made to avoid cutting through a town, a county, or a state.

With a few minor exceptions, the entire world operates on standard time meridians that are multiples of 15°; each zone in principle extends 7½° East and West, and differs by exactly one hour from the next zone.

From the fact that the 15° zones differ by exactly one hour you can infer that for each degree of longitude the difference in local time would be exactly four minutes.

Eastport (longitude 67°W), 8° East of the standard meridian, is 32 minutes fast on Eastern Standard Time. Washington (longitude 77°W), 2° West of the standard meridian, is 8 minutes slow on Eastern Standard Time. Savannah (longitude 81°W), 6° West of the standard meridian, is 24 minutes slow on Eastern Standard Time.

Put differently, local noon on April 15 falls at 12:00 noon at any place on the 75th meridian. On the same day it falls on 11:28 A.M. at Eastport, 12:08 P.M. at Washington, and 12:24 P.M. at Savannah.

The four-minute-per-degree-longitude rule is not hard to remember. To decide where it's earlier and where it's later, just remember that the sun rises in the East and travels West. So it'll get to Eastport before it gets to the 75th meridian; and it'll get to that meridian before it gets to Washington, Savannah, and all points West of it.

If one degree causes a four-minute difference in time, then one-quarter degree (15') will cause a one-minute difference.

To calculate your local time in standard time, first find your longitude—to the nearest quarter degree—from the top or bottom margins of the topo quad you are using. Compare that longitude with the longitude of the meridian of your standard time. In the United States, standard time meridians are as follows:

Eastern Standard Time 75°W
Central Standard Time 90°W
Mountain Standard Time 105°W
Pacific Standard Time 120°W

Say you are near Red Lodge, Montana, at longitude 109°20', rounded to 109¼°. That's 4¼° West of your standard time meridian (105°). Figure 4 minutes times 4 makes 16 minutes, plus one more for the quarter degree makes 17 minutes in all for the time difference.

You are West of the Mountain Standard Time meridian, so the sun gets to you later. It'll be local noon at your location 17 minutes after the time given in Table 11.3. If the table gives 12:03 P.M. for the time of local apparent noon, the sun will be due South of you at 12:20 MST.

The quarter degrees are easy when you use 15′ series topo maps. If you are nearer the right edge of the map, use the figure given in the right corners; nearer the left edge, use the figures from the left corners.

Daylight saving time adds another minor complication. You have to remember that *daylight saving time is fast time.*

The simplest way to deal with this is to add one hour to the time of local apparent noon.

In the above example, if you were on daylight time you'd have the sun due South of you at 1:20 Mountain Daylight Time.

Again, you don't have to carry the whole table. A few lines will cover a two-week trip. You may want to add the hour for daylight time as you make up your card.

The accuracy of the method is very good. The error of South found by this table, corrected for longitude, at any date before the year 2000 at least, is comparable in accuracy to that read from a base plate compass corrected for declination. The one exception is South of about latitude 37°N from May through July. In latitude 30°N, for example, you can expect an error of up to 3° in that period. Below that latitude the error increases rapidly.

Equal Altitude Method

You don't need accurate time, a table, or a knowledge of your longitude to use this method. Its only drawback is that it takes some time to wait for the result. It can be combined with a long lunch break.

The theory behind it is that the height of the sun above the horizon a given time *before* noon is virtually the same as it is the same interval of time *after* noon, everywhere and at any date.

In practice you measure the height by the length of the shadow. Before noon you mark the shadow the tip of some vertical object casts on a horizontal surface and measure the shadow's length from the base of the vertical object. When the shadow reaches that length again in the afternoon, you again mark it.

A line from the center of the base of the object casting the shadow through the point halfway between your two marks points directly North.

The difficulties for the wilderness traveler are the vertical object and especially the horizontal plane. But if you take a lunch break at an organized campground, a pencil, a piece of string, and a picnic table will let you demonstrate the principle to anyone who wants to wait, watch, and check with a compass. So would a ski pole and a frozen-over lake, or a flagpole with a paved area to the North of it.

Any error in the result is due to the crudeness of the tools, not the method. To satisfy the nit-pickingest critic I used the word *virtually* to qualify the sun's elevation before and after noon.

The difference is a very slender nit. At the worst periods of the year, around the beginning of spring and fall, the angle of the sun above the horizon changes by about one minute of arc per hour. For a two-hour ob-

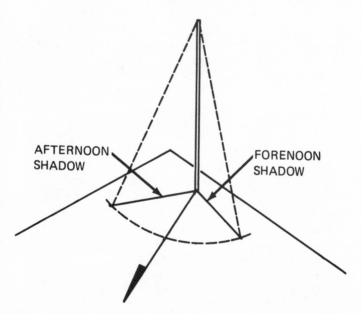

AFTERNOON SHADOW

FORENOON SHADOW

Figure 11.1 *Equal altitude method for finding North from the sun.*

servation period, that makes the shadow of a yard- or meter-high pole 1/16 inch (1 millimeter) longer or shorter.

Directions from the Stars

At night by far the best guide in the area under discussion in this chapter is Polaris, or the Pole or North Star. It gives North so accurately that you can use it to find the declination for your location. The traveler without compass does not need to pay attention to all the fine points of magnetic direction discussed in Chapter 8.

If you have forgotten how to find Polaris, Figure 11.2 illustrates one method.

Many people who would not call themselves experts on stars can recognize Orion with its hourglass shape, two very bright stars and three dimmer stars close together in a straight line (the belt of the mythical hunter, Orion).

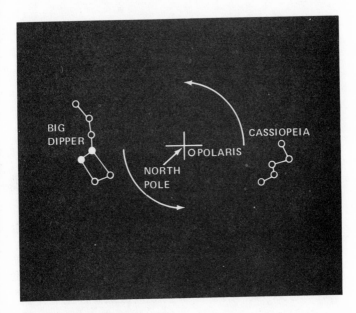

Figure 11.2 *Finding Polaris.*

The belt of Orion is almost exactly on the celestial equator and so rises everywhere due East and sets due West.

So you won't forget whether it's the first star to rise and set or the last, use the middle star. You'll be within one degree or so of true direction.

Again, as with the sun, you have several minutes at rising or setting in which the bearing hardly changes.

This is a simple emergency method with only one drawback. On some nights in summer Orion rises when it's already daylight and sets before it gets dark. At that time of year you must use other stars that rise (due East) or set (due West) during the hours of darkness.

There is no easy way to recognize a lot of stars and constellations. But you don't have to become an expert. There's one star that's not hard to find and that rises and sets during darkness when Orion is on vacation.

You find it with the aid of the familiar Big Dipper,

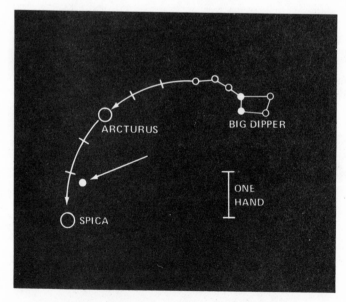

Figure 11.3 *Finding Zeta Virginis.*

as shown in Figure 11.3. Follow the arc of the handle for about three hands (arm outstretched). There you'll find a first-magnitude star (Arcturus). Continue your arc another three hands, and you'll come to another bright star (Spica in the constellation Virgo, the Virgin).

The star that interests us is between the two: about one hand from Spica, two from Arcturus. It's a third-magnitude star (about as bright as the dimmest of the five stars that form the W or M of Cassiopeia).

That brightness refers to the time when the star is well up in the sky. It seems much dimmer just before setting, just as the setting sun seems much dimmer than at noon.

The star has no common name; its official name is Zeta Virginis. It is difficult to recognize when it rises (due East), but when it sets, after you have seen it at full brightness, it gives you everywhere an accurate West.

Warning: planets sometimes play around near Spica; don't let them confuse you.

12.

Direction from the Sky: The Tropics and South of the Tropics

The preceding chapter showed ways for finding directions from the sky in latitudes north of the tropics. This chapter outlines some methods that can help you get directions in other areas.

Some of the astronomical facts underlying these methods are old hat to local outdoor people. But I'm mainly concerned with helping northerners who ski in Chile in what's summer at home, or who hike in New Zealand at Christmas.

The Tropics

The tropics are defined as the zone between latitude 23½°N and 23½°S, approximately. They are also de-

fined as the only zone on earth where the sun at noon
can be directly overhead. Throughout the zone that
happens on two days of the year. (At the borders with
the temperate zones the two days shrink to one.)

The tropics are also the only area on earth where
the sun for part of the year is on the "wrong" side of
the sky at noon. By that I mean it's sometimes North
of you in the northern tropics, South of you in the
southern.

Table 12.1 gives the approximate dates for which
that is true. For example at latitude 11°N between April
19 and August 25 the sun will bear North of you at
noon. At latitude 11°S between October 22 and February 20 the sun will bear South of you at noon.

On or near all the dates given in the table the sun
will be directly overhead at noon.

The length of day, important for planning winter
travel in higher latitudes, is of little concern in the
tropics. Days here vary by only about an hour from
the 12-hour yearly mean. But twilight here is shorter

Table 12.1 Direction of the sun at noon in the tropics

Latitude (degrees)	Latitude North, noon sun North	Latitude South, noon sun South
1	Mar. 24–Sept. 21	Sept. 26–Mar. 18
3	Mar. 29–Sept. 16	Oct. 1–Mar. 13
5	Apr. 3–Sept. 10	Oct. 6–Mar. 8
7	Apr. 8–Sept. 4	Oct. 11–Mar. 3
9	Apr. 13–Aug. 31	Oct. 17–Feb. 26
11	Apr. 19–Aug. 25	Oct. 22–Feb. 20
13	Apr. 25–Aug. 19	Oct. 28–Feb. 15
15	May 1–Aug. 12	Nov. 3–Feb. 9
17	May 8–Aug. 5	Nov. 10–Feb. 2
19	May 16–July 28	Nov. 18–Jan. 25
21	May 26–July 19	Nov. 27–Jan. 16
23	June 10–July 2	Dec. 12–Jan. 1

On or near all the dates given in the table the sun is directly overhead
at noon.

than in higher latitudes—barely long enough to pitch
the tent and boil water between sunset and darkness.

In the tropics compass needles should be balanced
for what Silva labels NME (the zone North of the
magnetic equator), or ME (the zone of the magnetic
equator, where the needle dips neither northward nor
southward). Even if your compass wasn't intended for
the right tropical zone, you can probably tilt it enough
to make sure the needle swings freely.

Directions from the Sun

The sun and watch method, described in the preceding chapter, and the shadow movement method are
useless in these latitudes. The method based on the
length of shadows before and after noon is valid, but
during much of the year the shadow will be too short
for accurate results.

To make up for these shortcomings, the sun in these
latitudes is very good for giving accurate direction at
sunrise and sunset. Your location hardly affects its
bearing. When the sun is about one-half its diameter
above the horizon at sea during sunrise or sunset, its
bearing is almost the same all through the tropics. (As
you can see from Table 12.2 the difference is never
more than two degrees, and often less.)

That may sound strange.

When it's midwinter at latitude 23½°N, the sun rises
well South of East and sets well South of West, just as
elsewhere in the Northern Hemisphere at the time of
the shortest days. But that's the time of midsummer at
latitude 23½°S. Here the sun also rises South of East
and sets South of West, but makes a long arc by way
of North, to make the longest days of the year.

Having thought that through, you may still be surprised that sunrise (or sunset) takes place on virtually
the same bearing over such a large area. It is truly vast,
stretching around the globe at its widest and more than
3200 statute miles from North to South. That's about
the distance from the Tropic of Cancer to the North
Slope of Alaska, well beyond the Arctic Circle.

Perhaps the Polynesians were guided on their epic
voyages by sunrise and sunset bearings. In the trade

winds you can trim sail to a given course, and some vessels will hold that course all day or all night.

The sailor has ample time to trim his sails, and the hiker need not worry about minor obstructions on the horizon. To change bearing by one degree takes the sun 10 minutes in latitude 23½°; 15 minutes in latitude 15°; 23 minutes in latitude 10°; and 46 minutes in latitude 5°.

The idea that the Polynesians may have navigated by sunrise and sunset bearings came to me during some single-handed sailing in the tropics. It was published in *Sky and Telescope* in June 1967. David Lewis, in the December 1974 issue of *National Geographic*, reported that he sailed his catamaran *Rehu Moana* from Tahiti to New Zealand by this method, without a compass or other navigational instruments.

His course, based on tradition, was "a little to the left of the setting sun in November." After 35 days he made a good landfall.

You probably plan no such voyage. But it's nice to know that in a pinch a card with a few lines of figures can give you accurate direction twice a day.

Directions from the Stars

In the northernmost tropics Polaris will guide you just as it does in higher latitudes, but the Big Dipper and Cassiopeia—always close to the horizon—disappear for long stretches.

Since Polaris is so close to the celestial North Pole, one would expect it to be visible down to latitude 0°. But, as mentioned in the previous chapter, celestial objects get dimmer near the horizon. About 5° above the horizon, Polaris appears as a fourth-magnitude star, which means that even with low humidity you'd only see it in the dark of the moon.

In his famous single-handed voyage around the world, Captain Slocum first saw Polaris again in latitude 7°13′N. He, of course, had a compass to show him exactly where to look. As a rule, you won't see Polaris until you are North of the latitude of the Panama Canal (9°N).

The stars in the belt of Orion are almost on the celestial equator. So all through the tropics they pass

Table 12.2 Bearing of sunrise and sunset in the tropics (in degrees)

Date	Sunrise Latitude, North or South		Sunset	
	0°	23½°	0°	23½°
Jan. 1	113	115	247	245
16	111	113	249	247
25	109	111	251	249
Feb. 2	107	109	253	251
8	105	106	255	254
15	103	104	257	256
20	101	102	259	258
26	99	100	261	260
Mar. 3	97	98	263	262
8	95	95	265	265
13	93	93	267	267
18	91	91	269	269
23	89	89	271	271
29	87	87	273	273
Apr. 3	85	85	275	275
8	83	82	277	278
13	81	80	279	280
19	79	78	281	282
25	77	76	283	284
May. 1	75	74	285	286
8	73	71	287	289
16	71	69	289	291
26	69	67	291	293
June 10	67	65	293	295
30	67	65	293	295

high above you. At rising and setting these three stars show East and West, as elsewhere.

If you are very observant, Orion will look a bit strange to you in southern latitudes—it's upside down.

Not only Orion but all constellations are upside down. So are the familiar markings on the moon. The waxing crescent moon looks waning, the waning crescent waxing. First quarter looks like last and last like first.

The moon in the tropics is a fine subject of conver-

Table 12.2 continued

Date	Sunrise Latitude, North or South		Sunset	
	0°	23½°	0°	23½°
July 1	67	65	293	295
19	69	67	291	293
28	71	69	289	291
Aug. 5	73	71	287	289
12	75	74	285	286
19	77	76	283	284
25	79	78	281	282
30	81	80	279	280
Sept. 5	83	82	277	278
10	85	85	275	275
16	87	87	273	273
21	89	89	271	271
26	91	91	269	269
Oct. 1	93	93	267	267
6	95	95	265	265
11	97	98	263	262
17	99	100	261	260
22	101	102	259	258
28	103	104	257	256
Nov. 3	105	106	255	254
10	107	109	253	251
18	109	111	251	249
27	111	113	249	247
Dec. 11	113	115	247	245
31	113	115	247	245

sation when you're snowed-in while tent-camping in Canada. It makes everybody feel warmer. However, you may not be believed if you repeat the statements I just made.

Prove them. Draw a crescent or our friend Orion. Then ask the doubters whether they believe that the farther south you go the higher above the horizon the moon and Orion will appear. They won't argue about that.

Eventually you come to a point where the moon, or Orion, is directly overhead. If you keep moving the drawing just a little farther, the shape of Orion and the apparent phase of the moon suddenly flip.

You can practice your magic act with this book. Raise it higher and higher until you have it above your head. Keep going a bit farther and you'll see the type and drawings upside down.

If after having used it a few times you can locate Spica and if necessary turn the constellation Virgo upside down in southern latitudes, you can use the method described at the end of Chapter 11.

There is no southern equivalent of Polaris, a star bright enough to be seen on a moonlit night and close enough to the pole to indicate South without a compass. The constellation Southern Cross is some help. While you can work with it part of most nights in the tropics, the method belongs to more southern latitudes and you'll read about it presently.

South of the Tropics

Athletes are often interested in latitudes south of the tropics, where the seasons are reversed. In Australia you can train for ocean swimming at Christmas. In Chile you can train through our summer for the Winter Olympics, not just on glaciers and slush but on freshly fallen winter snow. A man I knew who lived for fly fishing commuted regularly between British Columbia and New Zealand in his year-round search for record trout.

One consequence of the switched seasons is the length of day. The longest days in the Southern Hemisphere are around Christmas, the shortest around the Fourth of July.

To help you plan winter activities, Table 12.3 gives length of day for southern latitudes (During the warm season, October through March, the days are at least 12 hours long.).

You'll find the approximate length of day on the line of the nearest day in the column of the nearest latitude. For a margin of safety you may want to use the next higher latitude.

Example: On August 5 at latitude 45°S you find 9.8

hours, about 9¾ hours. The next higher latitude (52°S) gives about 9 hours.

You'll get a little more accurate results by interpolating values for dates and latitudes as described in Chapter 3. No calculations are needed, just rough approximations.

When the days are short compared to what you plan to achieve, don't forget to add the time before the start, and the time it takes to set up camp, when you plan the day.

Contrary to childhood fantasies, people in the Southern Hemisphere do not walk on their heads. But compass needles do dip the other way. In Australia and New Zealand, for example, they dip as much southward as they dip northward in the contiguous United States.

Needles are counterbalanced at the North end in southern latitudes to counteract this tendency. A Silva compass would be marked MS for Magnetic South. Compasses balanced for South America and southern

Table 12.3 Length of day in southern latitudes*

Date	Latitude				
	20°S	*35°S*	*45°S*	*52°S*	*56°S*
Mar. 18	12.1	12.2	12.3	12.4	12.4
29	12.0	11.9	11.8	11.7	11.6
Apr. 8	11.8	11.5	11.2	11.0	10.8
19	11.6	11.1	10.7	10.3	10.0
May 1	11.4	10.7	10.1	9.5	9.1
16	11.2	10.3	9.5	8.7	8.1
25	11.1	10.1	9.2	8.3	7.6
June 10	10.9	9.8	8.8	7.8	7.1
July 19	11.1	10.1	9.2	8.3	7.6
Aug. 5	11.3	10.5	9.8	9.1	8.6
18	11.5	10.9	10.4	9.9	9.5
30	11.7	11.3	10.9	10.6	10.4
Sept. 10	11.9	11.7	11.5	11.3	11.2
21	12.1	12.0	12.0	12.0	12.0

*Time between sunrise and sunset is given in hours and tenths of hours; one-tenth of an hour equals six minutes.

Africa are marked SME for South of the magnetic equator.

Directions from the Sun

The hour-hand method described in Chapter 11 works nicely near the South Pole during the roughly six months you can see the sun. Point the hour hand toward the sun. If you like, you can use the shadow of a match to help align the sun and the hour hand. South is then halfway between the hour hand and twelve o'clock on the dial.

In parts of Antarctica the errors of that method may be tolerable. But the errors get out of hand as you move toward the equator, just as they do in the Northern Hemisphere.

That puts most of the land masses of the Southern Hemisphere out of bounds for the sun and watch method. Most of them are in lower latitudes than one would guess. The southern tip of Australia is in the latitude corresponding to Atlantic City; Africa's southern tip corresponds in latitude to Los Angeles. The Strait of Magellan, which terminates South America's mainland, is in the latitude corresponding to that of Birmingham, England.

The shadow movement method for finding East is just as unreliable in the Southern Hemisphere as in the Northern Hemisphere.

The bearing of the sun when it rises or sets works here as accurately as in the Northern Hemisphere. You can use the tables in the preceeding chapter without any changes. And you won't run off the tables at high latitudes the way you do in Scotland, the Scandinavian countries, and much of Canada.

The method for getting direction from the sun at noon—local apparent noon to be precise—also works in southern latitudes. But the sun here invariably bears North at noon, making the shadow point South. Apart from that, use Table 11.3 and the instructions given with it. The method of equal altitudes, which needs neither correct time nor any tables, works just as well as it does in the Northern Hemisphere, again with the shadow at noon invariably pointing South. That makes

the mid-point between the shadow marks due South of
the object that casts the shadows.

Directions from the Stars

Polaris, that faithful night guide in northern latitudes, is invisible in the Southern Hemisphere. There is
no equivalent star near the pole of the southern sky.
The star nearest the celestial South Pole, which would
indicate South as truly as Polaris indicates North, is of
fifth magnitude, close to the limits of naked-eye visibility. You can see it only when the sky is free of both
moonlight and artificial light and if your eyes are totally adapted to the dark. Its official name is Sigma Octantis; it doesn't have a common name. Perhaps the
difficulty of finding it will spur some readers into looking for it.

To make the task easier here are a few clues. The
star will be due South of you, and as many degrees
above the horizon as you are from the equator. At latitude 30°S, for example, it'll be 30° (three hands, arm
outstretched) above the horizon.

On a dark, clear night, after your eyes have not
been exposed to a light—not even a match—for the
last half hour look for a star that fits this description.
Use a sighting compass corrected for local declination
to get the direction.

By coincidence, Sigma Octantis is about as far from
the celestial South Pole as Polaris is from the celestial
North Pole. That's roughly one degree, or half the
width one of your fingers covers in the sky with your
arm outstretched.

By another coincidence, there are two stars pointing
about as closely to Sigma Octantis as the two that
point to Polaris. Here the stars are at the end of the
long arm of the Southern Cross. Sigma is not quite
three hands from the nearer guide, which forms the
foot of the cross.

Unfortunately, when you find a star in the right location, it may still not be the right star. Unlike Polaris,
which stands away from all equally bright neighbors,
Sigma has a few equally dim siblings in the constellation Octans.

For the wayfarer without compass, that makes it a pretty poor guide star. But you already have a clue for finding approximate South from the stars in the constellation Crux, the Southern Cross.

Most people who see it for the first time are disappointed. It's not nearly as large as they had expected; it isn't quite square; and the stars are not all of the same brightness. Three of them are first-magnitude stars or almost so, but one at the end of the crosspiece is a third-magnitude star, dimmer than Polaris.

Sometimes novices conjure up another group of four stars and mistake it for the Southern Cross. Don't worry about that false cross. The true Southern Cross has two closely spaced, very bright stars (Alpha and Beta Centauri) nearby for positive identification. The crosspiece roughly points to these stars, which are on the side of the brighter end star.

Now you have the Southern Cross nailed down. Its long axis points (almost) to the celestial South Pole, 27° (a skimpy three hands) away in the direction of the foot of the cross.

You can check that. From the head of the cross (the star nearer the crosspiece) to the foot is about six degrees, or three fingers. The distance to the pole is about four and a half times that.

The point you'll get by drawing this straight line continuing the long axis of the cross misses being due South of you by about three degrees. That's much better than no direction at all.

The Southern Cross does not remain visible all night and every night until about latitude 37°S. But even near the Tropic of Capricorn it will guide you about three-quarters of the time.

The big surprise for most northerners is that you don't have to cross the equator to see this famous constellation. It's clearly visible, though low on the horizon, from Key West in the evening in April and May.

If you use the method of measuring the scant three hands in the direction of the long axis Key West, you'll end up at a point in the water. But that point will be amazingly close to being South of you. I have used this method with good results while sailing through the Bahamas.

That means, of course, that you can also use this method in the tropics when the Southern Cross is in the sky.

Orion will be upside down all through the Southern Hemisphere, but quite recognizable. It will give you a reliable East when the belt stars rise, West when they set.

So will Zeta Virginis, which is described in detail at the end of Chapter 11.

Here's an aid for finding Spica, the bright star in the constellation Virgo that will help you locate Zeta Virginis. When the space between the two bright stars, Alpha and Beta Centauri, and the Southern Cross bears South of you, Spica will be North of you. Look for Arcturus somewhat East of North. Arcturus, the other star used for finding Zeta Virginis, bears North when Alpha and Beta Centauri bear South, about an hour later.

13.

Land Navigators' Tricks

Orienteering is a sport about which you may never have heard, unless you have friends who are interested in it. Then you may have heard more than you ever wanted to know about it.

Orienteering as a competitive sport is generally a combination of jogging—uphill and downhill—and land navigation at its most demanding. Several books have been written about it, such as *Orienteering,* by Hans Bengtsson and George Atkinson (The Stephen Greene Press, Brattleboro, Vermont, 1977).

I could pretend not to be the competitive type. But there's a much more truthful reason why I don't indulge in that sport. On the speed scale of hare, through rabbit, to bunny—I'm a tortoise. And a tortoise has as much business among these harey types as a donkey in the Derby.

Occasionally orienteering courses are set up just for noncompetitive types. On these you can proceed at your own speed, smell the flowers, or identify the birds. The only requirement is that you finish the course—typically a two-mile (three-kilometer) loop—in time for the committee to get home for dinner.

There is a polite name for the noncompetitive people who amble through the woods finding perhaps a half dozen control points with map and compass: "wayfarers."

True competitors are quite properly called runners. Unfortunately, they are also known as orienteerers, which reads like a misprint. Worse, they are sometimes called orienteers.

By whatever name, these types use some interesting terms that you may add to your navigational vocabulary. And they use techniques of navigation you may find useful. Many of them are not new of course. But they make a nice mixed-up starter kit for your own stuff sack of tricks.

In the usual competitive meeting the runners are given a map on which from 7 to 15 control points are marked. The runners must find them—by whatever route they choose—in the proper order and in the least possible time.

The actual control point is identified by a bread-box-sized red-and-white kite-shaped structure. You won't see it until you are quite close. To prove you have visited each control, you mark your card with a punch or colored pen provided there.

Competitors start several minutes apart so they can't just follow the runner ahead, but have to do their own navigation.

The course setter strives to avoid "comers" at any control getting clues from "leavers." But one wonders if one clever definition of the sport, "running with cunning," refers only to the skill with map and compass.

In some ways the participants in an organized meeting have it easier than individual hikers.

The maps used are redrawn so that magnetic North is at the top. That eliminates the problem of allowing for declination in figuring courses and taking bearings. (So, of course, does a compass with declination adjustment, once it is set for the area.) And North-South lines, close enough for you to catch one under your compass no matter where you place it, are already drawn for you. Also, the map is on a larger scale than regular topo maps; 1:15,000 is common.

The map is field checked just before the meeting. Abandoned trails are removed; so are torn-down buildings. New structures are added. Marshes that have dried up since the original topo map was made are left off, cliffs that didn't show between contour lines are drawn in, and so on.

How can you get into the sport of orienteering? Perhaps the reference librarian at the nearest public library can tell you.

Or write, enclosing a stamped, self-addressed, long envelope, to Orienteering Services/USA, P.O. Box 1604, Binghamton, New York, 13902; or Orienteering Services/Canada, Inc., 3345 North Service Road, Burlington, Ontario, Canada L7N 3G2.

Cross-Country Travel

By the nature of things, much competitive running is cross-country.

Most other outdoor people stick to trails most of the time. One author estimates that 90 percent of all travel is on trails. I think his estimate is low, especially when you count individuals rather than groups. A solo hiker is more likely to strike out through the bush than is the leader of a group.

In some places nobody should leave a trail, even for a few steps. The most obvious places—though still not obvious for some—are the turns at switchbacks. A single hiker cutting across can start erosion that will grow with every heavy rainfall and will create two gullies in the trail, one above and one below the turn.

Other places where one must stick to trails include subalpine meadows, tundra, and peaks. In all these places boot-scarred vegetation takes years to heal.

Moist, low-level forests, the usual setting for orienteering meets, recover quickly from off-trail hiking.

Few sane people will abandon a trail for a bushwhack without good reason. I did once in North Carolina. We were walking downhill on a dirt road—a *track* in orienteering language—along a creek. When the road swung away from the creek I had a brilliant idea: "That's the creek that crosses the main road farther down. Why don't we just follow the creek till we come to the bridge?"

"Is there a trail?"

"It's less than a mile by the map."

At first there was a fishing trail. Then we hopped from stone to stone. Then bushes and trees closed in and we had to detour through a marshy area. After two hours a blowdown of trees stopped us cold.

William Kemsley Jr., founder of *Backpacker* magazine, tells in *The Whole Hikers Handbook* about bushwhacking on the shoulder of Table Mountain in the Catskills. It took his party eight hours to thrash its way through roughly two miles of fir thicket.

Such examples should discourage the bravest would-be bushwhackers. Books on orienteering give some rules of thumb, such as the following, for estimating time expended on various types of ground to cover the same distance:

Type of terrain	Time units
Roads or good paths	1
Tall grass	2
Forest with light underbrush	3
Forest with thicker underbrush	4–6

In the western United States and much of Canada there are vast open areas where off-trail walking is fairly easy and does no permanent harm to the vegetation.

But the rule still holds: don't trade a trail for a bushwhack lightly.

Perhaps you have no intention of ever leaving trails. But someday, somewhere, you may find yourself obviously off the trail. The usual advice is to retrace your steps. But that's sometimes not easy to do. Everybody will tell you not to panic in such a situation, perhaps throwing in some advice on distress signals.

I suggest a calculation. Say it took five minutes before you realized you were no longer on the trail. That assumes your feet were in an impossibly deep trance; otherwise they would have let your brain know about it sooner.

How far can you be from the trail? At two miles (three kilometers) per hour, you can't be more than 300 yards (250 meters) away. Even with your spaced-out feet.

Did you walk uphill, level, or downhill in the last few minutes? Did you walk into the sun, with the sun at your back, or to the left or right? Was the wind ahead, behind, or on your left or right? If you can recall any of that, you narrow the search area enormously.

When you go scouting for the lost trail, don't leave your backpack behind. You risk finding the trail but losing the pack.

The effort of finding a trail lost 300 yards back will almost everywhere be less than that required to bushwhack to an unseen destination—or even to one that's visible.

Some trails end abruptly. Game trails, for example. If you carried a rack of antlers on your head, wouldn't you follow a path in the trees that's clear of obstructions? That avoids headaches. But when you come to the edge of the meadow, you'd graze here and there, leaving no permanent spoor.

Often trails seem to end abruptly where soft ground changes to rock.

Break out your binoculars and look, at first, in the direction you have been walking and somewhat left and right of that. Perhaps you'll spot a pyramid of stones—a cairn or duck—to show where the trail continues.

If its builder followed the book, there should be a long stone parallel to the trail on top.

If you are not sure what you see is such a marker, or if you start out hunting for one, make sure you can find the spot where the trail ended if you must retrace your steps. Walk a compass course rather than making a grazing-cow search.

Route Planning

Let's look over the shoulder of a runner as he decides on the course from the start to the first control point.

He'll almost certainly reject the beeline. A good course setter is not likely to arrange for such an unimaginative leg. Also, most courses are run in hill country and that eliminates most beelines; they'd go up one side of the hill and down the other. You don't gain as much time on the downhill leg as you lost in the uphill struggle. So up-and-over is longer and harder than staying level or nearly so.

Staying level means following a contour of the land, a contour line on the map; so following such a course is known as *contouring.*

Even though most of us don't worry much about time on the trail, only children and dogs have extra energy to spare. When you carry your house, bed, kitchen, wardrobe, library, and other stuff on your back, every foot not climbed is a foot gained.

Long ago, while ski touring, I learned the Law of Conservation of Energy for backcountry travelers: never give up elevation needlessly. That can become quite an obsession. I find myself muttering at trails that without apparent reason make me climb and then go down again.

Orienteering runners don't carry packs—except perhaps a pack of chewing gum—but they too avoid uphill work. Orienteering books mention the following formula: 1 foot (or meter) uphill equals 10 to 12½ feet (or meters) on the level over comparable ground. You can substitute hiking with a load for running. Obviously that formula can apply only to moderate grades, not vertical walls.

The climb itself is easily estimated from the contour interval of your map. On our map the interval is 40 feet, so three intervals equal a detour of 1200 to 1500 feet. On the Kompass maps of the Alps (1:50,000), with a contour interval of 100 meters, a climb of one interval is worth a detour of 1 to 1¼ kilometers over comparable ground.

The runner planning his route to the vicinity of the first control avoids runs by compass. Instead he looks for a *handrail*.

This descriptive orienteering term, means a long, mapped feature parallel to the direction of travel serving as a navigational aid.

A road or trail is too obvious an example; phone lines, railroad tracks, fences, and borders of fields and meadows can also act as handrails. So can natural features: valleys, ridges, streams, shores of lakes, and edges of marshes.

If you have digested earlier chapters, you'll recognize all of these features as potential position lines. But handrails is a much more vivid term.

You know how difficult it is to estimate distance in the landscape. What the runner needs is another position line to tell him when to abandon the handrail and turn left or right.

Such a position line in this sport is called a *catching* (or *collecting*) *feature*. This mapped feature, more or less across your direction of travel, has to be easy to recognize. It can be any one of the features listed for handrails, or a side stream, a crossing or merging trail, a building, and so on.

In your own off-trail work you may not always find a convenient collecting feature on the map just where you need one. But there often is—the bearing on some prominent peak, for example. Try to choose a bearing at about a right angle to the handrail you're following.

That's the *beam bearing* of coastwise navigators, who routinely change course when, say, an identified headland is abeam (meaning at right angles to the course). If your course is 30°, the headland—or here your peak—is abeam when it bears 120° (right) or 300° (left). The method wastes time in competitive running, but that hardly matters for hikers. With compasses of the mirror-sighting type and with the peak or other target not far off, the method is surprisingly accurate. It's most unlikely that the control you're looking for is visible from where the two position lines—handrail and catching feature—cross. Except perhaps on a wayfarers' course, the management is not that kind to competitors.

On courses for advanced beginners to experts the controls are progressively harder to find. The competitor tries to find a handrail and a catching feature to get him to a point near the control. From that point, the *attack point,* he proceeds by micronavigation to the control itself.

The controls are not only shown on the map, but each competitor has a brief description of each. Most descriptions are straightforward: trail junction, stream crossing, building, for example. A circle, its center at the exact position of the control, is drawn around it on the map. You can pinpoint the control from the offset of the circle relative to the building, trail junction, or other described features.

A few map features with descriptions peculiar to the sport are shown in Figure 13.1. At first glance some symbols look alike. But study them closer: a pulpit juts out; at a spur the contours jump in and out; at a reentrant they form a fishhook shape, and so on.

When for lack of a suitable handrail runners have to fall back on compass courses, they use a technique they call *aiming off.*

Nobody can run a compass course with absolute accuracy. When you come to the catching feature but can't see the target, you don't know whether to look for it to the right or the left. If you deliberately aim off to the left, however, you know your target should be on your right.

A typical example for noncompetitive aiming off is getting back to your parked car by compass. You know the exact spot on the map where you left it. The road is your catching feature. Lay a course deliberately to one side of the direct one. Until by experiment you have found a formula that fits your style better, bear off about 10°.

That adds about 18 percent to the length of your walk. If that sounds like quite a price to pay, weigh it against the fifty-fifty chance of searching in the wrong direction and having to backtrack along the road to start the search on the other side.

The method was used by old-time mariners, and it's

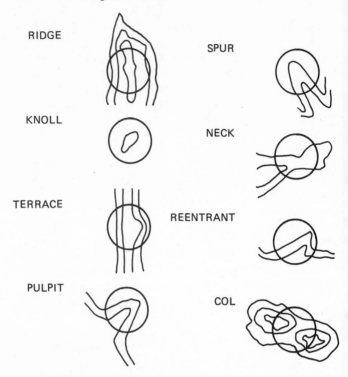

RIDGE

SPUR

KNOLL

NECK

TERRACE

REENTRANT

PULPIT

COL

Figure 13.1 *Control points commonly used in orienteering competitions, code names, and corresponding contour lines.*

still practiced on cruising yachts. Like earlier sailing masters, the captain doesn't flip a coin to decide on which side to approach, say, a harbor entrance. There's only one winning side: upwind or upcurrent. It'd be silly to have to work back against wind or current when you can get a free push.

On skis you'd approach your car on the uphill side, then ski down to it on the road. In competitions the runners also aim for the high ground, which usually gives a better view of the elusive controls.

Obstacles

Getting around unexpected obstacles is not a technique often demanded from competitive runners. Their maps are supposed to be so detailed and up to date that there's no room for the unexpected. And they are so smart they'd allow for expected obstacles in laying their course.

But how about us less smart ones with nothing but years-old topo maps to guide us?

You already know how to continue a compass course across, say, a creek too wide to jump and too deep or swift to wade. First you find a landmark—perhaps a prominent, odd-shaped tree—on the far side of the creek. You then search for a crossing and walk to your landmark on the far side. You resume your original course at the landmark.

A variation on that technique involves changing course to one side by a certain angle for a certain distance; you then change course by the same angle in the opposite direction and for the same distance. When the distance is up, you resume the original course.

You can see from Figure 13.2 that the two methods are really one. In the first version, the landmark serves to measure the distance.

In the second version, you must somehow estimate the distance. The standard procedure at sea is to time how long you spend on the first leg of the detour, and turn onto the original course when you have been on the second leg for the same length of time. On land it'll only work if slope and terrain on both legs are about the same.

On land, counting steps (or paces) is another possibility. I'll talk about that presently.

The angle to turn from base course is up to you. Two ships meeting head-on or nearly so might both turn 10°. At a creek you might turn 90°. To avoid an unmapped lake created last spring by a busy beaver you might turn 40°.

The Bézard compass, popular in Europe, has auxiliary marks 45° from the gate where you box the compass needle. On a 45° detour you simply box the needle first on the mark to right of North, then on the mark to the left. When you have traveled the second leg for as long as you traveled the first, you return to the standard mark.

If you want to try that system you can make your

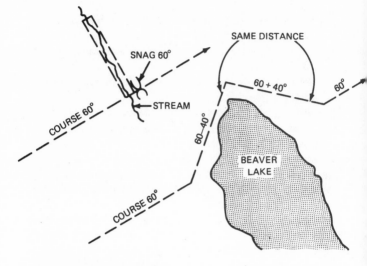

Figure 13.2 *Navigating around obstacles. Top: two 90° course changes. Bottom: two 40° course changes.*

own auxiliary marks by attaching bits of colored tape to the capsule of a plain protractor compass to box the needle at 45° and 315°. (That may not work permanently on some compasses with declination adjustment.)

Skiers use a special trick for making switchbacks in poor visibility. It could just as well be used by a group of hikers or snowshoers.

You make switchbacks when the direct approach is too steep. As long as you can see your destination, say a marker on the peak, there's no problem. You suit the angle at which you deviate from the direct course to fit the conditions. But in poor visibility you can proceed by course and distance using the following trick.

Change course 60° from the direct course. Measure your progress on that course. Then turn to 60° on the other side of the base course. When you have covered the same distance as on the first leg, you're again on the base course line.

Since you changed course each time by 60°, you have stepped out a triangle with all three sides the same length. In other words, you know where you are on the original course line.

You can use avalanche cords knotted together to measure the distance. The first member of the party makes a mark in the snow, the last member calls out "One" when he comes to the mark. When he hears the call—relayed if necessary—the leader makes another mark, and so on. (A piece of colored paper to be picked up by the last member of the party could be used in summer hiking.)

When your zig distance equals your zag distance, you can repeat the pattern or continue on the other side of the base course.

Since the two legs off the base course equal the distance gained along the base course, you have reduced

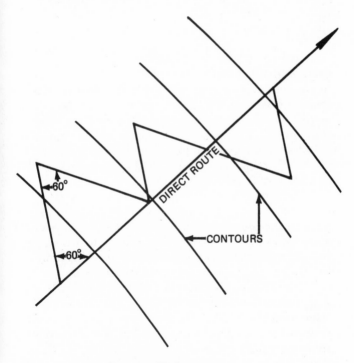

Figure 13.3 *Sixty-degree switchbacks.*

the slope to half its steepness. But sometimes that's not good enough on skis. Try 70° to one side or the other for reducing the slope to one-third its steepness. The distance made good toward your destination along the base course will then be two-thirds of the distance of each leg.

Here's a nautical trick you may find useful someday. Normally the helmsman is given a course and tries to make that course as closely as possible. When the ship's head has been blown off to the right by the wind, or pushed off by a wave, he'll steer to the left of the course for a while, hoping all the errors will cancel out.

Now suppose there is a hidden shoal to the right, open water to the left. The order may then be: "Course 180°, nothing right." That tells the helmsman to take all his errors to the left. When, for whatever reason, the ship takes off toward the right, he'll bring her back quickly and favor the left longer than the ship's excursion took.

Walking a compass course, we may have to zig around a rock here, zag around a fallen log there. An experienced hiker, like an experienced helmsman, will come out close to the planned course by making his zigs balance his zags.

Now it could happen that in poor visibility you have to ski a compass course. There are some nasty cliffs on your right. Give yourself the course, say 180°, and add "nothing right."

You may end up making good a course of 175°. So why not just use that course? If you are navigator and helmsman in one, it matters little. But if you are giving the course to another member of your party, the nautical order is shorter, clearer, and certainly better than saying, "Try for 175°, approximately, but—if anything—favor your left side, because there are some dangerous cliffs on your right."

Here's another nautical trick that may someday be useful to you. Suppose you are walking toward a distinctive landmark, say the monument on a peak. You are not quite certain where you are, but you surely want to avoid the mapped marshy area.

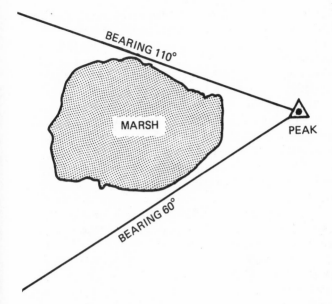

Figure 13.4 *Danger bearings.*

Draw lines from the peak that just miss the edges of the swamp. Then measure with your compass the bearings along these lines toward the peak. Say you get 60° and 110°.

You can approach the peak from any direction and be certain to avoid the swamp as long as the peak bears less than 60° or more than 110° from you. You can see from Figure 13.4 that you'd pass South of the marsh when the bearing of the peak is less than 60°. You'd pass North of the swamp when the bearing is more than 110°.

Following the Route

The runners in competition want to know at all times where they are. To do that they carry a map, folded and in a plastic map case, the direction of travel facing forward, one of the runner's thumbs indicating the present position.

Carrying the map oriented to the landscape makes eminently good sense for competitors. One of them—John Disley, the author of a book on the sport—figures that aligning the map with the terrain takes a minimum of 15 seconds; if the compass is needed for that operation, the time becomes 30 seconds, and the rhythm of running is broken.

Even when time is not important (what backpacker would refuse a half-minute rest?), carrying the map so it matches the landscape is a good idea. Someday it'll save you the embarrassment of having taken the left fork in the trail when clearly you should have taken the right one.

Keeping the thumb on the map is the equivalent of the navigator in an automobile keeping his index finger on the last landmark passed. But it's quite tiring. If you have better things to do with your hand, highlighting the trail you plan to take helps. Yellow felt-tip marker pens, which won't obliterate the detail over which you draw, are sold in stationery stores.

Highlighting your route will save you time whenever you consult your map. Better yet, it'll save you from navigating in a valley parallel to the one you're really in, or on a parallel ridge.

One way of keeping track of your progress is by remembering the time when you passed some landmark. Some people even follow nautical practice and pencil the time on the map, the way navigators record the time when they pass a buoy.

That means pulling the map out of its case or plastic bag. And for some of us even a wristwatch is too much civilization to carry into the wilderness. To me, the alternative—measuring progress by continuous counting of paces—is even worse.

Perhaps there is a time for counting paces and a time for carefree ambling. Again, we can learn from the competitive runners. They divide the course to each control into three sections, which require three different forms of navigation: rough, standard, and precision. Some call them rough compass (or rough map), standard compass, and so on. Others refer to a code of signal lights: green, amber, and red.

You have navigated in a similar way in an automobile every time you tried to find a street in a strange city. At first, rough navigation on main highways or interstates to the city limits or the proper exit. Then standard navigation to find the main thoroughfare you were told to look for. And finally counting city blocks or traffic lights to find the side street.

Running with a handrail allows maximum speed with a minimum of navigation. Clearly a green light, rough compass section.

When you are approaching the collecting feature the amber light goes on; you had better look for some intermediate mapped points or you'll miss the attack point. That's clearly a case of standard map-and-compass work.

From attack point to the actual control usually means proceeding by direction and distance—a red light, precision map-and-compass job. Here pace counting is the only way for measuring the distance.

A pace means a double step. You count one each time you put your right foot down. Or your left one, if you prefer. It's an ancient method of measuring distance.

Our word *mile* comes directly from the Latin for 1000 (paces). Enough Roman milestones have survived in place into modern times for us to know that a Roman mile was about 1618 yards (1479 meters). That's about 8 percent shorter than the statute mile of 1760 yards (1609 meters).

Some authors think the difference is due to the smaller stature of the Romans. Maybe the Romans carried more gear than the British. Or perhaps the legions marched in a more relaxed style.

There's no doubt that Roman paces were measured on good and level footways. Most of us would make paces of about 5 feet (roughly 150 centimeters) on such a track, as long as we weren't carrying appalling loads.

Competitive runners under the same conditions are said to average 7½-foot paces (roughly 225 centimeters). The runners measure their own pace on different slopes and different footways. If they had time to calculate all these variables while their brains are being bounced about, this method would be very scientific.

To make their task easier, many of them use gauges that let them measure distances on the map in their pace length. They need different gauges for the different scales of maps used at competitions (1:10,000, 1:15,000, or 1:20,000).

For hikers and other topo map users, 1:24,000 is the most likely map scale of interest. Assuming a 5-foot pace, how would you calibrate such a gauge? You'll recall that on this scale 2000 feet equal 1 inch. That makes 400 paces per inch, or 100 paces equal to ¼ inch. A strip of paper labeled as shown in Figure 13.5 and glued to an edge of your compass makes a simple gauge.

You could use the same gauge with negligible error with 1:25,000 maps. For a pace 150 centimeters long on such a map, the 100 pace marks would be exactly 6 millimeters apart.

That's your clue for 1:50,000 maps, much used in Canada, the Alps, and the rest of the world. The 100-pace marks should be exactly 3 millimeters apart.

On the 1:62,500 (or 1:63,360) maps, one inch equals about 1000 paces, an easy figure to remember. (The exact equivalents are 1042 and 1056 paces.)

You can use these gauges on paths that aren't level and smooth if you work out your personal factors. Measure on the map as usual. Say you get 400 paces.

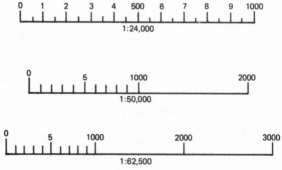

Figure 13.5 *Pace gauges.*

From earlier tests you know it takes 50 percent more steps through the woods without a trail. So you won't reach your destination until you have counted 600 paces.

Runners use a gadget, often attached to the compass, that helps them remember the count. For example, you can click the thing every time your count reaches 100, then start a new count.

Only you can decide if the counter, which adds several dollars to the compass sold without it, is worth it to you. Perhaps you could fold a finger for each hundred paces. Or move a match from one pocket to another.

The classic way of counting is with pebbles (*calculi* in Latin, which gave our language the words *calculation* and *calculus*). But who wants to lug pebbles around? Sunflower seeds are lighter.

Even without miscounting by 100 paces, don't expect great accuracy from counting paces in steep or rough terrain. In the rather tamer conditions of the competitions, even experts don't expect to get less than 10 percent error.

While we're on the subject of accuracy and error, you may want to know how far off you'll be sideways when walking a compass course. You have read how to translate angular error into feet or meters at the beginning of Chapter 8, "Magnetic Direction." But many of us often deal with percentages, so perhaps that kind of figure is easier to remember and apply.

Don't expect to do better than a 5 to 7 percent error. That means you'll likely be 50 to 70 feet (or meters) off after walking 1000 feet (or meters). That figure is based on a generally agreed on error of three to four degrees. It includes errors of the compass and of the person who carries it. It applies to walking in the open, not dodging around boulders and detouring around undergrowth in the forest.

And it's only for a one-way trip. If you make a round trip by compass (to retrieve something you lost, for example), you may miss your present position by twice that; allow for a 100- to 140-foot (or meter) error for the round trip over a 1000-foot (or meter) distance.

Slope and footway are not the only variables that affect distance and direction estimates. How can one keep track of a slope that changes rapidly or terrain that varies every few minutes?

Here's a typical example. You approach a lake on a well-trodden path. To reach the upper end of the lake you hop from one tuft of sour grass to the next for a while. Then, where a creek runs into the lake, you run into a stretch of sucking mud, followed by a rock slide. Next you have to climb steeply to get around a cliff that drops sheer into the lake. On the top of the cliff fallen trees slow you down. What factors do you apply to these pace counts?

To make life easier and pace counts more realistic, competitors use a simple trick. They look for mapped checkpoints along the route and start a new pace count at each. Passing the abandoned mine, or crossing the mapped creek, you know where you are much more accurately than a pace count could tell you.

You'll soon find out where it pays to count paces—say, for finding a spring—and where you might as well eat the sunflower seed.

This conscious looking for checkpoints has a built-in bonus for noncompetitive hikers. It helps you find the way back. You may have no intention whatever of returning the way you came, but sometimes the mountain gods laugh at your plans. A weather change, a minor injury, or a swollen stream may force you to return the way you came. New navigators make a startling discovery at this point: the way back looks completely strange.

Occasionally the very opposite happens. One member of your party is willing to swear that this is the snag where he tied his shoelace on the way in, there is the rock on which he rested his pack, and so on. A case of perfect recall for things never seen before.

The checkpoints you used on the way in may still stick in your memory on the way out. I also strongly recommend that you stop from time to time and look back. It adds to your enjoyment, and if you have to return by the same route, the scenery will not look strange.

Carrying the images of the return trail and check-points in your mind will alert you when you are some-where you aren't supposed to be.

How can we all be so stupid as to get off the trail? A level side trail has branched off just where the main trail changed slope abruptly. Or for some reason the main trail grows faint just where a side trail takes off. Other people who got sucked into the same trap may have made the false trail very noticeable. No wonder: they walked it coming and going, while they only walked once on the correct trail.

Orienteering maps show areas that are out of bounds for the competitors. Others must use common sense. Don't trespass on private land. Don't walk across cultivated areas. In some parts of the world that includes meadows.

In other areas you're quite welcome to walk through fenced land as long as you leave the gates the way you found them. Of course, you would close a gate you had found closed. But some strangers think they do the rancher a favor by closing a gate someone has left open. Don't do it. You may cut off grazing cattle from their water supply, or keep well-trained horses from coming home.

Don't smoke while crossing private land. In fact don't smoke—not even a pipe—while on the move. It'll taste twice as good in camp.

One last suggestion: try to memorize the general lay of the land through which you're traveling. Often there's only one map for an entire group. Many maps have dropped out of pack pockets or have been left far behind; and once I saw one take off in the wind and sail out of sight.

Just knowing in which direction the road to civiliza-tion may roughly lie could be a help.

You may have heard the advice, "Follow the drain-age when lost." The idea is that water runs downhill, ending up in bigger and bigger streams near which people are likely to live.

The logic is sound, and despite occasional lakes and waterfalls encountered, may get you out of the bush better than spinning the bottle. But the overall mental map here too is a great help. Otherwise, in the Canadian Rockies for example, you might follow a drainage that leads to the Beaufort Sea.

Index

Italic numerals indicate illustrations; tables are indicated by the letter T